Judy Upton

Plays: 1

Ashes and Sand, Stealing Souls, Sunspots, People on the River, Know Your Rights

Judy Upton's first play *Everlasting Rose* was produced at the London New Play Festival in 1992. In 1994 she won the George Devine Award for *Ashes and Sand* (Royal Court Theatre Upstairs) and the Verity Bargate Award for *Bruises* (Royal Court Theatre Upstairs, 1995). Her other plays are *Temple* (The Room, Richmond Orange Tree, 1995); *The Shorewatchers' House* (The Red Room, Kentish Town, 1996); *Stealing Souls* (The Red Room, 1996); *Sunspots* (The Red Room, 1996); *People on the River* (The Red Room at the Finborough, 1997); *To Blusher With Love* (winner of the 'Open Stages competition: Channel T.C. at The Man in the Moon, 1997); *Pig in the Middle* (Y Touring, schools tour and the House of Commons, 1998); *The Girlz* (The Room, Richmond Orange Tree, 1998); *Know Your Rights* (The Red Room at Battersea Arts Centre, 1998); *Confidence* (The Door, Birmingham Repertory Theatre, 1998); *The Ballad of a Thin Man* (Channel Theatre Company tour, 2000) and *Sliding with Suzanne* (Royal Court Theatre, 2001).

Also by Judy Upton and available from Methuen

Bruises/The Shorewatchers' House

Confidence

JUDY UPTON

Plays: 1

Ashes and Sand
Stealing Souls
Sunspots
People on the River
Know Your Rights

Introduced by the author

Methuen Drama

Methuen Contemporary Dramatists

1 3 5 7 9 10 8 6 4 2

This collection first published in Great Britain in 2002 by
Methuen Publishing Limited
215 Vauxhall Bridge Road, London SW1V 1EJ

Ashes and Sand first published in 1995 by Methuen Drama
in *Frontline Intelligence 3: New Plays for the Nineties*
Ashes and Sand copyright © 1995, 2002 by Judy Upton
Stealing Souls copyright © 2002 by Judy Upton
Sunspots copyright © 2002 by Judy Upton
People on the River copyright © 2002 by Judy Upton
Know Your Rights copyright © 2002 by Judy Upton
Introduction copyright © 2002 by Judy Upton

Judy Upton has asserted her rights under the Copyright, Designs and
Patents Act, 1988, to be identified as the author of this work

Methuen Publishing Limited Reg. No. 3543167

A CIP catalogue record for this book is available
from the British Library

ISBN 0 413 76060 X

Typeset by SX Composing DTP, Rayleigh, Essex

Printed and bound in Great Britain by Cox & Wyman Ltd, Reading

Caution

Contents

Judy Upton
A Chronology

June 1992	*Everlasting Rose* (London New Play Festival, Old Red Lion, Islington)
December 1994	*Ashes and Sand* (Royal Court Theatre Upstairs)
April 1995	*Temple* (The Room, Richmond Orange Tree)
October 1995	*The Shorewatchers' House* (The Red Room, Kentish Town)
November 1995	*Bruises* (Royal Court Theatre Upstairs)
April 1996	*Stealing Souls* (The Red Room)
May 1996	*Sunspots* (The Red Room)
June 1997	*The People on the River* (The Red Room at the Finborough)
September 1997	*To Blusher With Love* (The Man in the Moon/Worthing Ritz)
February–May 1998	*Pig in the Middle* (Y Touring, schools tour and the House of Commons)
March 1998	*The Girlz* (The Room, Richmond Orange Tree)
May 1998	*Know Your Rights* (The Red Room at Battersea Arts Centre)
September 1998	*Confidence* (Birmingham Repertory Theatre)
February 2000	*The Ballad of a Thin Man* (Channel Theatre Company)
September 2001	*Sliding with Suzanne* (Royal Court Theatre Upstairs)

Introduction

Plays produced in fringe theatres tend to be overlooked when theatre history comes to be written up – despite the fact that many early plays by the current crop of younger playwrights were put on in venues above pubs, arts centres etc. There is also a kind of snobbery that decrees that once a writer has had work on away from the fringe, then that's where they should stay. It is often assumed that an established writer will only have a play produced at a fringe venue because a mainstream theatre has rejected it. It is simply not true. There are all kinds of reasons for working on the fringe, from having greater artistic freedom and needing to respond to an issue quickly to wanting to work with a particular company or director.

With the exception of *Ashes and Sand*, all of the plays in this volume were produced by the Red Room Theatre Company. Launched in October 1995, by Lisa Goldman and Emma Schad, it has consistently developed work with a critical and original take on the world we live in. Starting life above the Lion and Unicorn pub in London's Kentish Town, their first production was my *The Shorewatchers' House* (also available from Methuen). This plus three other plays in this volume were directed by Lisa Goldman – part of our long-term artistic collaboration.

In this volume, *Stealing Souls* is a one-act two-hander set in Brazil, and was influenced by my reading of South American literature. It might be described as English magic realism meets S&M love story.

With *Sunspots* it's back to the English seaside to explore the relationship between two sisters, and the idea that two people can grow to complement each other like two halves of the same whole. It transferred to Battersea Arts Centre, and the fact that it had a pizza in the final act kept an impoverished writer fed for many a night.

People on the River was a Red Room commission – an attack on victim TV and media exploitation.

Know Your Rights – my first attempt at writing monologues – was part of a rapid response political season, where a number of writers responded to the media's uncritical complacency where the new labour government was concerned. While examining litigation culture I was also looking at a wider issue: the powers that be and the way in which they encourage us to blame those immediately around us when things go wrong, in order to prevent us seeing the bigger picture.

Finally, back to *Ashes and Sand* – a take on girl gangs and shoe fetishism in Brighton. This play is also about the frustrations of being a working-class teenager, seeing the very limited prospects that are coming your way and dreaming of escape.

These plays were my escape. I hope you enjoy them.

Judy Upton
November 2001

Ashes and Sand

for my family

Ashes and Sand was first performed at the Royal Court
Theatre Upstairs, London, in association with the Royal
National Theatre Studio on 1 December 1994. The cast was
as follows:

Glyn	Richard Albrecht
Lauren	Rakie Ayola
Hayley	Susan Lynch
Anna	Samantha Morton
Young Man	
Doctor	
Store Detective	Michael Parker
Psychologist	
Man	
Daniel	Nick Reding
Jo	Melissa Wilson

Directed by Ian Rickson
Designed by Jeremy Herbert
Lighting by Johanna Town
Sound by Paul Arditti
Music by Peter Salem

Setting: Brighton, the nineties

Act One

Scene One

Only the back of the stage is lit. Sounds of sea, gulls, passers-by, arcade machines. A **Young Man** *is standing slouched against a railing, his back to us. He sips from a can of Sprite and scratches his arse. Four teenage girls –* **Hayley**, **Anna**, **Jo** *and* **Lauren** *enter and stand in a huddle.* **Hayley** *walks up to the oblivious* **Young Man**.

Hayley Hallo.

The **Young Man** *turns to face her.*

Hayley Mmmm. You *are*.

Young Man Sorry?

Hayley Seriously gorgeous. We saw you from the wheel.

She is centimetres from his face, smiling, leaning in for a kiss. The **Young Man** *leans back, tries to look round her at her still huddled friends. Suddenly, on impulse he puts his arms around her and gives her a kiss.*

Anna Woooo!

Jo More.

Hayley *angles for a proper kiss. The* **Young Man** *drops his hand for a fistful of thigh, lifting her skirt. The huddle of girls moves in and engulfs them, as their mouths meet. A furious mass of DMs and flying fists. The* **Young Man** *collapses groaning.* **Jo** *has his wallet. The girls run off.* **Hayley** *returns and crouches by the prostrate* **Young Man**. *She stands up and kicks him in the head.*

Lights down.

Lights come up, front left. **Daniel** *(twenties) and* **Glyn** *(thirties) are playing darts.* **Daniel** *in a suit,* **Glyn** *in a police uniform. Across the dartboard a pin-up of a woman, which has obviously been there for some time. The bull's-eye is her cunt.* **Daniel** *is the better player.*

Glyn   Carol's twisting my arm to invite you to dinner this week.

Daniel   Ah . . . very busy I'm afraid.

Glyn   Gemma's crazy mad for you, it's over with Josh from tumble tots. Says she's going to marry you for ever and ever.

Daniel   Friday.

Glyn   Friday evening, yeah.

The **Young Man** *wanders in holding a blood-covered hanky to his face.*

Glyn   Hallo.

The **Young Man** *groans.* **Daniel** *pushes the dazed* **Young Man** *into a chair by the desk. He picks up a huge sheaf of papers.*

Daniel   So tell me about it.

Lights up back of stage.

Hayley *and* **Anna** *are standing by a wheeled shoe rack, prominently marked with huge red and white sale stickers.* **Anna** *is plastering them with more stickers.*

Hayley   Bali.

Anna   The Azores.

Hayley   No. Bali. Listen.

She produces a page torn from a travel brochure.

'Bali – The Morning Of The World. Dramatic landscape, golden sandy beaches, a unique culture and some of the friendliest people you will ever be fortunate enough to meet.'

Anna   Where?

Hayley   Nineteen hours away.

Anna   How much?

Hayley   We've four hundred and twenty-three quid.

Anna   That all? We ought to do more tourists.

Hayley (*poking out her tongue*)   French?

Anna *pokes out her tongue too and they move together in a mockery of a kiss recoiling at the last minute.*

Hayley   Ooooh, garlic!

Anna   Look at these.

She holds up a pair of naff court shoes.

Hayley   Seven ninety-nine, who are they kidding?

Anna   Some sad slapper'll buy 'em, and I'll flog her some shoe polish and a pair of extra-long laces.

Hayley   You're hoping.

Daniel *walks past the girls without them noticing him. He appears to have a number of items hidden under his coat. He walks to the front of the stage and sits down on a bed front right. Beside it is a long dressing table and mirror. Candles on the dressing table turn it into a kind of shrine.* **Daniel** *unbuttons his coat and lots of ladies' shoes fall out on the bed. He takes a crumpled piece of paper from his pocket, picks up the phone and dials the number.*

Daniel (*uncertainly*)   Is Rebecca . . . oh hello! Sorry didn't recognise . . . Daniel, Danny. You gave it to me. You did! The arcade . . . ah you *do* remember. Thank you, that's a nice thing to say. Stop laughing. I can't hear you properly. Are you busy – homework? They don't. Have you got time for a chat. I have, yeah. So, talk to me. I don't know. What do you like! Can't think? Hobbies . . . you don't. Get a life! Tell me how school was today. I bet. Your parents then? Is he?

While he is chatting on the phone, **Daniel** *takes off his shoes and socks, unbuttons and rolls up his sleeves, undoes and starts to slide down his trousers.*

Yeah, mine too, at my age. That's mums for you, Becky. You don't, huh? What then? Reba . . . Reba! That's really nice, really pretty, and sort of raunchy. You're welcome.

He lies down and pulls the duvet over himself. The shoes fall on the floor.

Good one? A wild party. Hayley? Yeah, not the Hayley I know. Oh maybe then. That sounds like something she'd . . . No, no, just a friend of a friend of.

Knock on the door. **Daniel** *jumps.*

Someone at the door. I should be so lucky. No, have you? Boyfriend, I mean. Well, there is someone . . . no . . . no! Alright, her name's Gloria. Yes she is, well, I think so.

Thumping on the door.

Shit. I gotta go, sweetheart. Take care. Yeah, let's make it soon, babe. Must go. Bye.

Daniel *does up his trousers, kicks the shoes under the bed and goes to the door.* **Glyn** *is there.*

Glyn   Thought I'd drop by –

Daniel   I'm really very busy.

Glyn   Got a girl down the nick – Whittaker. Hayley Whittaker. One of a little posse pulled in about the guy that got steamed on the pier. All innocent eyes and butter wouldn't melt, except her. Said they could all go home, but she won't go unless you come down and talk to her.

Daniel   What aftershave are you wearing? Improvement on the usual.

Glyn   Christmas present from Carol. If you're gonna marry, marry one with class.

Daniel   Tropical fish. Saw a tank and filter in the free-ad paper. Over here. Do you think?

Glyn Tina on the desk used to have some guppies and neons and things. So how do you know this girl?

Daniel Tina?

Glyn Whittaker, Hayley.

Daniel Her dad. Clay pigeons. Gotta do something about my hair. And this place's a mess.

Glyn Wait till you have kids. Smells you won't believe.

He comes right in.

I bet you even dust under the bed.

He checks and pulls out a woman's shoe.

Daniel Sandra's.

Glyn Recent?

Daniel No.

Glyn Don't think I –

Daniel We keep in touch.

Glyn No hard feelings then? That's nice. Are you coming?

Daniel In my pants?

Glyn To see this girl.

Daniel Girl?

Glyn Whittaker –

Daniel – Hayley. She just wants a lift home in a panda. You're the man to give her one . . . in a manner of speaking.

Glyn I think it's your truncheon she wants to feel.

Daniel (*quickly*) What's she saying?

Glyn Come see.

Daniel Appointment, ten minutes, sorry.

Glyn   Woman?

Daniel   Run her home. Say I said 'Hallo'.

Daniel *fetches his coat and goes out past* **Glyn**. *Lights up back of the stage.* **Jo**, **Anna** *and* **Lauren** *are gathered around the arcade machine. They make room for* **Daniel** *to sit on the stool in front of it. He starts to play the game. The girls put money in.*

Jo   Fuckin' fast fingers.

Daniel   Someone's been telling stories. Shit. Crashed. Another life I've lost. So where's Hayley this evening?

Anna   Dunno.

Jo   Jealous, Anna?

Daniel   Another one bite the dust. Want a go, Lauren?

Lauren *has been staring into the distance. She starts.*

Daniel   Come sit on my lap.

She does.

There.

He guides her hands on the controls.

Relax. Wait for it to start. There're your lives. Still seeing Marty?

Lauren   No, I –

Daniel   Right concentrate! Left! Up! Here we go. Slowly. Watch out! Quick, jump! Jump again. Good.

Lauren   You're breathing in my ear.

Daniel   Is my breath hot?

Lauren   Yes. You're licking . . .

Daniel   I'm not. I'm not touching you, am I, Jo?

Lauren   My ear feels wet.

Daniel   It's only my breath condensing on it.

Lauren   Shit, you've made me crash.

Anna   Don't blame Danny. You're just crap.

Lauren *jumps off* **Daniel***'s lap.*

Lauren   God, you randy fucker.

Daniel   Excuse me.

Exit **Daniel**.

Anna   Should we tell him?

Jo   About our plan? No, he's a pig. I mean, he's a nice bit and all that, but he's still a bastard whatever way you look at it.

Anna   Fuckin' pigs. Hayley won't tell him anything.

Jo   Course she won't, fucking kill her.

Jo *takes out her flick-knife.*

Anna   Call that a knife? Hayley'd have that off you in seconds.

Jo   Like to see her try.

Jo *takes up a combat position.*

Lauren   Daniel's coming back.

Jo *puts the blade away.*

Jo (*to* **Daniel**)   Better, darling?

Daniel *sits down.* **Lauren** *slides back on to his lap.*

Jo   You only have to ask. I'll always give you a blow.

Daniel   You'll be the death of me.

Anna   You want to come round Thursday night. Mum has to work. We could watch a film or something, have a nice time. I'll take care of you.

Jo   I'll be there too. Like a little orgy, darling?

Daniel   Wish you'd all talk to me like you used to.

Lauren   Tell you all our secrets?

Daniel   You don't trust me.

Lauren *squashes his nose with her finger.*

Lauren   Cos you're a pig.

Daniel   A big pink one.

Jo   Show us.

Anna   Come on, darling.

Daniel   Want to get me arrested.

Jo   Yeah.

Daniel   Talking of which do you really think I don't know what's going on.

Jo   Pig.

Daniel   This pig don't squeal, so don't you think you might trust me a little? You used to, and I never let you down.

Anna   I don't trust anyone now.

Jo   What you don't know won't hurt you.

A car alarm goes off, distant.

Anna   Let's put him to the test. Shall we?

Daniel *nods.*

Jo   One, two, three . . .

Jo, **Anna** and **Lauren** *sprint off. After a moment* **Lauren** *returns to* **Daniel**. *Sounds of the girls yelling, laughing and kicking a car, windscreen smashing, etc., offstage.*

Lauren   Jo and Anna are so immature sometimes.

Daniel   They've sent you back to keep an eye on me.

Lauren   No!

Daniel   It doesn't matter.

Lauren   On a Tuesday, after school if I've been, I go to the rec. You know that little wooden shelter in the middle. I just sit there and smoke or something. You ought to come by . . . God, are you listening, Danny?

Daniel   Do you still go down the gym?

Lauren   Three nights a week. The whole gang do. You could meet us down there sometime. Feel my muscles.

He feels her upper arms.

It's a jungle out there. Survival of the fittest and all that.

Daniel   Are you eating OK, Lauren?

Lauren   My hips are still really big.

Daniel   Lauren, you are not fat.

Lauren   Fuck off.

Daniel *wanders along to the place by the railings where the* **Young Man** *stood before he was attacked.* **Daniel** *takes up the same position.*

Daniel   You think I don't know everything that goes on? What's Hayley's 'plan'?

Lauren   Ask her.

Daniel   I will. Where are the Azores anyway?

Lauren   Up your arse.

She pinches his bum.

Have you seen Hayley's little book? She's got all sorts of plans in there. Like dreams, only she always gets what she wants.

Daniel   Always?

Lauren   You better believe it.

She rubs her back up against **Daniel***'s.*

I'm just warning you so you know.

Daniel   Know what?

Lauren   God, you're stupid sometimes.

Lauren *turns and leans on him. She strokes his hair.*

Lauren   You've gone quiet.

Daniel   Do you know how many muscles it takes to smile? Sometimes it's exhausting. I don't want to smile any more.

Lauren   Then don't.

Daniel   I don't want to be touched any more.

Lauren   Yes you do.

Daniel   I don't want company.

Lauren   Oh sure.

Daniel   I've applied for a job in Gibraltar.

Lauren   What do you want to go there for? The sun? What about the Azores?

Daniel   What about them? Is that where your family are going this year?

Lauren   No. So when are you going then?

Daniel *shrugs.*

Lauren   Don't go, Daniel. I know it sounds soft and everything but we care about you.

Daniel *hugs her.*

Daniel   You don't know me.

He releases her abruptly and walks off.

Lights down back of stage. Lights up front of stage. **Hayley** *is crouched at the front of the stage, one sleeve rolled up, bleeding cuts criss-cross her arm.*

Enter **Anna**. **Hayley** *quickly rolls her sleeve down.* **Anna** *sets a six-pack of beer down on the floor.*

Anna   Alright? What happened with the pigs?

Hayley   Nothing. They wouldn't tell Daniel I was there. I waited about half an hour. Wasted my time. Why wouldn't they get him? I started kicking a chair about. Should've kicked somebody's arse. God, why do those bastards look down their noses at us? Are they laughing? Do you think Daniel talks to them about us?

Anna   Men always like to get together to slag you off. Men are the biggest bitches in the world. He was down the arcade earlier.

Hayley   Doing what?

Anna   Talking to us. Me, Jo and Lauren.

Hayley   Watch Lauren, she'll stab you in the back. What was he wearing? Let me build the picture in my head.

Anna   Grey trousers, ecru shirt. Boots and his hair kind of wind-ruffled . . .

Hayley   Was he wearing *that* smile? Oh forget him. I don't want to know. I'm not going to see him again, ever. I hate him. How much did you spend –

Anna   I don't know.

Hayley   Money that was to take us to Bali. You spent it on him.

Anna   Only a few quid, Hayley. I'll pay back every penny when I get my wages.

Hayley   Let's go out. Let's spill some blood.

Anna   Time of the month?

Hayley   PMT. I feel angry. If I don't hurt someone I don't know what I might do.

Anna   Shall we go on the pier?

Hayley   No, he might be there. Let's go to the precinct.

She fetches a rounders bat. She puts on her jacket and puts it up the sleeve of it. She makes up her face looking in a hand mirror. **Anna** *brushes* **Hayley***'s hair.*

I look awful. I look like an old tart. I'm going to be sixteen soon – fuckin' Jesus, that's old. By the time I'm twenty, I'll need a facelift.

She shakes up a can of beer.

Anna.

Hayley *sprays the beer over* **Anna**.

Anna   You bitch!

Anna *chases* **Hayley** *offstage.*

Sounds of police sirens. Lights up back of stage. **Glyn** *is setting out road cones around a dimly lit, apparently headless corpse.*

Enter **Daniel**.

Daniel   Jesus.

Daniel *crosses himself.*

Glyn   Suicide driver. Going to have to scrape him up in a dustpan. My sixth stiff this week. They say life is cheap these days but it costs a fortune clearing up after the recklessness of youth. I reckon some of the innards and other bits we bag up, end up in the cat food. In America they have road-kill cafés – serve up flattened rats and stuff. Only one step from cannibalism – and why not?

Daniel *takes off his shirt and throws it over the head end of the corpse.*

Glyn   Did they cough up for your dry-cleaning last week, Dan?

Daniel *fetches some flowers. He lifts the corpse's hand, places the flowers on its chest with the hand holding them in place.* **Glyn** *takes a* *piece of chalk from his pocket, starts drawing an outline around the corpse.*

Glyn   I wonder if seeing so many traffic snuffs and suicides is what's making me impotent. Do you think? Had a blazing row with Carol last night, over nothing really. She says that I hate her dad. Actually I hate *my* dad. He wants to marry again. He's seventy-one.

Daniel   How's Gemma?

Glyn   She's drawn you a picture, of a caterpillar with boots on floating in the sky. Must be something they put in their milk.

Daniel   I won't be able to make dinner on Friday. Double-booked.

Glyn *picks up a road cone and holds it to his crotch, thrusting crudely.*

Glyn   Give her one for me, whoever she is. Anyone I know?

Daniel   No.

Enter **Hayley** *unobserved. She kneels beside the corpse.*

Glyn   Oy!

Hayley   Where's his head?

Glyn   Can you get her out of it?

Daniel   Come here.

Daniel *takes hold of* **Hayley**'s *arm and drags her to her feet. He pulls her downstage.*

Hayley   You're rough and ready tonight.

Daniel   Take me home.

Hayley   I don't know where you live, you'll never tell me.

Daniel   I'll tell you while you're driving.

Glyn   Danny . . .

Glyn *starts to come over.*

Glyn   Don't happen to have another bit of chalk . . .

Hayley   Driving what? I'm fifteen, I don't have a car.

Daniel   Well, go and nick one, can't you? I'll only be a few minutes here.

Blackout.

Scene Two

Front of stage left. A white-coated **Doctor** *is talking to* **Daniel**.

Doctor   A week ago, Detective Sergeant McClune, you came to me for an independent medical examination required for a job transfer . . . I've been unable to satisfy myself, what I mean is I don't think I can give you a clean bill of health without being completely sure that . . . the injuries you've sustained . . . in the line of duty have not caused any lasting internal problems . . .

Daniel   So you want to cut me up to see how I manage to hold together?

Doctor   I think a couple of X-rays and a barium meal will suffice. The radiographer can fit you in in half an hour. OK?

Daniel *nods. He picks up an executive puzzle from the desk, turns and peers at it.*

Doctor   So . . . whilst on duty you've been shot once and stabbed three times.

Daniel   Yeah.

Doctor   How do you feel about it? Does it play a large part in your desire to leave these shores?

Daniel   No, it's nothing to do with that.

Doctor I think . . . I will also have to recommend a psychiatric report alongside the medical one. The kind of experiences you've had must've left some emotional as well as physical scars. Have you had much counselling?

Daniel *shakes his head.*

Doctor Do you often talk about what happened, with friends, loved ones, colleagues?

Daniel No, not really.

Doctor Do you feel comfortable talking about your injuries and how they were sustained?

Daniel Yeah.

Doctor The first one was the shooting?

Daniel Yeah.

Doctor How did . . .

Daniel (*matter-of-factly*) Pursuing a suspected TDA. Car stopped, asked the driver to get out. Took a gun from his pocket, shot me in the shoulder.

Doctor And then shortly after you returned to your duties, you were stabbed for the first time.

Daniel *opens a tube of mints. He eats one.*

Daniel Domestic dispute. I got between the husband and wife. She tried to lunge at him around me, lost her balance, grabbed her wrist but she stabbed me with a pair of scissors, almost severing my left nipple. Suppose it's had some psychological effect in that it's made me wary of scissors. Don't get my hair cut as often as I ought to.

Doctor And then three months later.

Daniel A woman was brought in our nick, a vagrant, she was very drunk at the time. Because she was virtually comatose when they brought her in, they hadn't bothered to search her. Got a bit stroppy, I had to help my colleagues restrain her. She had a flick knife and she stuck it through my arm.

Doctor   Right through? . . . Oh yes, you showed me.

Daniel   Third time? Early morning, went with a couple of colleagues to make an arrest. The guy's girlfriend was screaming blue murder. It was quite funny really. Had the carving knife, standing there in a green shiny basque – old and fat, enormous tits though, you should've . . . anyway she says 'I'll stick it in, I "f"-ing will.' 'Do it,' I said . . . and of course . . .

Doctor   Right. Ah . . .

Daniel   It didn't hurt that last time. I was completely relaxed. Maybe that's why. Left side again, quite low down. I watched her push it in and pull it out again. It felt . . . warm, that's all, almost comforting, just a tiny twinge in the base of my spine . . . like . . . like I don't know . . . I collapsed but I felt . . . I don't know, relieved of my guilt, can you understand that?

Doctor   Yes, yes . . . of course. The psychologist could see you Tuesday, Thursday maybe.

Daniel   I'm very busy this week.

Doctor   The next then, Monday?

Daniel   Maybe I should ring you when I know what my shifts are.

Doctor   OK, fine. All three stabbings by women. Do you think that's affected your relationships . . . I notice you're single, you're a young man but do you think . . . er . . .

Daniel   I haven't become wary of women. I know what's happened to me is unusual – violent attacks on police officers by women are statistically low and to happen three times to the same officer must put me in a somewhat unique position, but there it is. And . . . and they weren't the sort of women I . . .

Lights up, back of stage. **Hayley** *is scrutinising a car radio-cassette, recently ripped from a car, wires still dangling.* **Jo** *looks on.*

Jo   Is it any –

Hayley   Fucking old junk.

Furious **Hayley** *slings the radio off.*

Here.

She gives **Jo** *a couple of pounds.*

Get yourself a copy of *Which?* Learn it all up. Which car stereo! Which TV! Which video! Don't bring me any more shit! Which car was it?

Jo   A white one.

Hayley *shoves her.* **Jo** *shoves* **Hayley** *back.*

Jo   A white Micra.

Hayley   You won't find a halfway decent stereo in a Micra, you stupid slag. New jacket? You've tons of jackets.

Jo   Old ones, crap ones.

Hayley   That's money that could've gone into our fund. That's Bali you're wearing on your back. Have you got the receipt? Get a refund.

Jo   No way. I'm not walking round looking like a bag lady. I'll need some nice gear for Bali. If it really is paradise I wouldn't enjoy myself if my clothes were all horrible.

Hayley   You won't need a jacket in Bali. It's boiling hot, you retarded cow!

Jo   I haven't decided if I'm going yet. First it was bloody Azores this, bloody Azores that, and now it's Bali, Bali, Bali. Fuck Bali. I might want to stay here and get a job or go to college or something.

Hayley   There's a man. I know it.

Jo   Well, there's Marty.

Hayley   Lauren's Marty.

Jo   They split up last week so it's OK.

Hayley *grabs* **Jo** *around the throat.*

Hayley   You slipped in while the bed was still warm. Don't you ever do that to me, not ever, Jo.

Jo   Daniel?

Hayley *laughs.*

Hayley   Still having the party Friday?

Jo   Left it a bit late to get the drinkies.

Hayley   We could do the offy now. Borrow Theresa's brat and buggy. You should've bought a jacket with seriously huge pockets.

Jo *takes a handful of chocolate bars out of her pockets. She gives one to* **Hayley**. **Hayley** *puts her arm around* **Jo**, *they walk off.*

Lights on downstage.

Lauren *is sitting on the bed listening to a personal-stereo.* **Glyn** *and* **Daniel** *burst in.*

Lauren   Shit! Get out! Mum. Mum! Did you let the pigs in? Hey, have you got a warrant? You can't just come barging in, I might be undressed or something. Is that what you want to see? Are you some kind of perverts?

Daniel *makes faces at her over* **Glyn**'*s shoulder. She winks at him.* **Glyn** *starts to look around the room.* **Daniel** *sits down on the bed.*

Lauren   You shouldn't have come here. The neighbours'll think I'm a grass. They'll do our windows, they'll trash Mum's car.

Daniel   Lauren, you've been identified as one of a gang involved in vandalism and theft from vehicles in the precinct.

Lauren   Who said?

Daniel   You were identified?

Lauren   What's, what's he doing? He's going through my things!

Glyn *picks up a pair of shoes.*

Glyn   Do you have a receipt for these?

Lauren   Expect I've chucked it out.

Glyn   Expensive shoes.

Daniel   Try 'em, Glyn, look nice with your little black number.

Lauren   Got a friend, Anna, who works in a shoe shop, gets us all the seconds cheap. I don't nick stuff, I'm not stupid.

Daniel *picks up a pop magazine and flicks through it. He starts humming a hit by one of the bands. He picks up a make-up compact and, unnoticed, pockets it.* **Glyn** *hovers, awaiting instructions.* **Daniel** *indicates 'go ahead'.*

Glyn   Think one of us ought to have a word with the mother?

Exit **Glyn**. **Daniel** *flops out on the bed.*

Daniel   Hard day.

Lauren *rubs his back.*

Daniel   To continue with our questions. Ahhh, what's your star sign?

Lauren   Aries, but I'm not a typical Arian . . .

Daniel   Favourite film star?

Lauren   Most fuckable? Johnny Depp. Aren't you going to search me?

Daniel   A woman officer has to do that.

Lauren   You could pretend, couldn't you? So why did you become a pig if you can't mess around with female suspects? Seriously, Danny, why did you decide to become a policeman?

Daniel *opens a packet of mints. He puts one between his lips and offers it to* **Lauren**. *She takes it in her lips.*

Daniel   I ought to make up a story about how my parents were killed by robbers, so I decided to avenge their deaths and . . . that's how it all happened for Batman apparently. Or maybe he just liked dressing up.

Lauren *opens a make-up compact and looks in the mirror.*

Lauren   He wanted a disguise. I can understand that.

Daniel *is flicking through the magazine.*

Daniel   Look at her!

Lauren *snatches the magazine.*

Lauren   She's fat. You like fat girls? No, I don't buy it. I can see through your bullshit if others can't. I know what you're trying to do, but I have been eating. I have. Not that it matters much. Fat or slim someone like me's never going to look like that.

Daniel   You're much prettier than her.

Lauren   Oh sure. But look at those clothes, you can't find anything like that in our high street. And she can go anywhere dressed like that, all the best clubs and parties. What hope for me of a life like that? Hayley reckons it's possible, that all it takes is money and she thinks we can make that kind of money. But I can't see it, we've been talking about going away somewhere exotic for three years. When's it going to happen? I've been offered a job at last. Washing up in a restaurant – crap.

Daniel   You have to start somewhere, I suppose.

Lauren   It's no good starting somewhere that's going nowhere. There's nothing for people like us, nothing. I thought I was having Marty's baby, but I'm not. If I had my first kid now while there's nothing else on offer maybe I could get a good job when I'm older, too old for stupid youth schemes, old enough to get some respect. You haven't got any kids?

Daniel   You know I haven't.

Lauren   I don't, even you probably don't know for sure that you don't – do you? Would you like to be a father, Danny?

Daniel   No way, forget it, Lauren.

Lauren   I wouldn't name you on the forms, unless you wanted me to. You wouldn't have to pay. Think about it?

Daniel   No.

Lauren   Is it because of Hayley? Are you in love with her?

Daniel   No.

Lauren   No? Oh my God! But you and her . . . I mean, you're shagging her and everything.

Daniel   I'm not shagging Hayley. Don't look at me like that. Have another mint.

Enter **Glyn**.

Glyn   Call for assistance, off-licence in the square.

Exit **Glyn** *and* **Daniel**.

Lauren   Mum! Mum, I'm going out, all right?

Exit **Lauren**.

Lauren (*off*)   *Whoooo, hooo!*

Back of stage, **Jo** *and* **Anna** *are doing exercises as if in a gym.*

Lauren (*entering*)   Hey you guys.

Jo   Hey yourself. Come to burn some of that fat off your thighs, Lauren?

Anna   Guess what?

Lauren   What?

Anna   We're in the money!

Jo   You'd better believe it, darling.

Lauren *sits down and starts doing sit-ups.*

Anna   Bali this autumn.

Jo   One more lucky hit or a couple of smaller ones and we're there.

Lauren   That off-licence that was raided, hey that was never . . .

Anna *motions a halo over her own head.* **Jo** *points both fingers at herself.*

Anna   Jo and Hayley *are* Thelma and Louise.

Jo   We only went in there for a couple of bottles of plonk, but there was a nice guy on the counter, quite a looker actually . . . I acted thick about needing to choose some lager for Marty's birthday. The guy came over and started telling me all about the alcohol content of Canadian this and New Zealand that . . .

Anna   And the stupid prat left the till unlocked.

Jo   We get outside and I say to Hayley, 'Where're the bottles?' Usually you can see a few bulges. She hadn't bothered about the vino, she'd got nearly four hundred in fives and tens.

Anna   I'm going to go on the leg press. Keep count for me, Jo. Let's blitz those flabby bits for Bali.

Front of stage. **Daniel** *lights the candles. He puts a woman's shoe on the dressing table as if on an altar. He takes a shoebox full of make-up and a mirror from under the bed and puts on lipstick.*

Daniel *picks up the phone and dials a number.*

Daniel   Hi, Carol. Is Glyn . . . OK.

He blows a kiss at his reflection.

Danny, yeah. Have you ever had to see a psychologist? No
. . . for my job in Gibraltar, they want a kind of psychological
profile. Probably because I've been carved such a lot.

He picks up pen and paper. He takes notes.

Just give short answers, what 'yeah' or 'no'? And big pauses,
what about that? I know it's stupid but I've been getting
myself in a real state about this. Yeah. Almost been thinking
of dropping my application. I can't explain. It's just . . . it's
just, oh I don't know, perhaps I'm just scared of what he
might show me about myself. You wouldn't? Yeah but
you're not like me, you're a family man. You just think
basically I'm overreacting and it'll be nothing to worry
about? Honestly?

There's a knock on the door. **Daniel** *wipes his mouth.*

Hallo, someone at the door. Girlfriend? I should be so
lucky. Probably my mum.

More urgent knocking.

Thanks, Glyn, yeah I do feel better about it now. Love to
Carol and Gemma. Yeah, I'm disappointed at not seeing
her too. Maybe next week, huh? Hope things are a little less
hectic.

More insistent knocking on the door. Loud thumping on the door.

You can hear that? Breaking the bloody thing down. Kids
messing around most like. I will!

Hayley (*off*)   Danny!

Daniel *covers the receiver to try to stop* **Glyn** *hearing* **Hayley**.

Daniel   Until tomorrow then. Bye.

He puts the phone down.

Hayley Danny! I know you're in. Hey!

She continues to bang on the door.

Open the fucking door! I need to see you! I need to talk! Now! OPEN THE FUCKIN' DOOR! OPEN IT! OPEN IT!

Daniel *stays where he is.*

Hayley I'll stay here until you do. Have you been talking to Lauren? She's lying to me, says you said things about me, about us. Did you talk to her? Did you? Just tell me. If you come to the door, or lean out of the window, I'll go away. I'll piss off straight away, Danny. That's if you want me to. If you want I'll come in. If you don't answer I'll sit here all night. Don't think you're going out anywhere, OPEN THE DOOR YOU BASTARD!

A **Psychologist** *comes in and sits on the desk, front left.*

Psychologist . . . for example, Freud believed that a fear of the dentist actually stems from childhood guilt about masturbating.

Daniel *walks over and sits in a chair.*

Psychologist But I think what I was trying to say to you is that we all have fears, all sorts of fears, both rational and irrational. I would be interested in knowing what fears you have, Daniel. I may call you Daniel?

Daniel *is clearly ill at ease.*

Daniel Yeah.

Psychologist (*coaxing*) What are you afraid of?

Daniel Ah . . . nothing . . . I mean, I don't know.

Psychologist Death perhaps?

Daniel No. Not any more than anyone else.

Psychologist Physical pain? Suffering: spiritual, er, metaphysical. You know what I mean by . . .

Daniel   Yeah. No, I don't worry about things like that.

Daniel *picks up a phallic-shaped desk toy from the top of the desk. He turns it in his hand, then hastily puts it down, self-conscious, anxious that it might tell the shrink something about him.*

Psychologist   Are your fears perhaps more abstract in their nature? Do you worry about letting others down?

Daniel   Sometimes maybe.

Psychologist   Of not living up to their expectations?

Daniel   Yeah.

Psychologist   Sometimes it's like living a lie. You fear being found out . . . Being exposed . . .

Daniel (*carefully*)   Maybe. No.

Psychologist   You fear betrayal.

Daniel (*quickly*)   Betraying myself . . . or being betrayed by others?

Psychologist   You tell me.

Daniel   I . . . I don't know.

Silence.

Psychologist   Well now, can we talk a little about your reasons for wanting to take this job in Gibraltar?

Daniel   Sure.

Psychologist   What makes you want to leave these shores, Daniel?

Daniel   I'm sick of the rain. I went to Gibraltar on holiday once and liked it. It's time for a change. Sometimes a thing crops up, the chance to take your life in a new direction, but it doesn't happen often. I bore easily, like surprises, I want my future to hold something I can't predict.

*The **Psychologist** nods and smiles.*

Daniel   Do you believe dreams can be . . . premonitions?

Psychologist   Dreams have always been seen to hold a significance, whether as messages, allegories or warnings. Freud, for example, and also Jung to an extent, subscribed to a view . . . that is they generally supported a notion which put forward the theory that –

Daniel   But what do *you* think? . . . I mean, what's your opinion?

Psychologist   I'm interested in what you think.

Daniel   I'm no expert, I –

Psychologist   Dreams often focus directly on our anxieties and taboos. Things we may find difficult to face or examine in the light of day.

Daniel   What things? You mean things like . . . I don't know . . .

Psychologist   Things like sex . . . and death for example.

Daniel   Things that are going to happen?

Psychologist   And things that have happened. Things we might, for one reason or another, want to forget.

Daniel   Yeah. But the future . . .

Psychologist   You've dreamt that your future lies in Gibraltar? Well, let's hope so. I wish you every success with your application.

Daniel *looks uncertain.*

Daniel   Is that it?

Psychologist   Yes, I think so.

Daniel   Oh . . . right . . . Thanks . . .

Back of stage.

Anna *is pricing shoes on a rack.* **Jo** *is watching her.*

Jo I don't know why you bother.

Anna I'm going to get a better job soon.

Jo Supervising somebody else sticking labels on shoes?

Anna No . . . I've got plans, if we don't get to Bali that is.

Jo Reckon we will?

Anna Hope so.

Jo Reckon we'll ever see any of that money Hayley's stashed away?

Anna What're you saying? Hayley would fuck us around?

Jo She'd better not, darling. How long have you known her, Anna?

Anna Oh years really. We've always been friends. Hayley's always been Hayley, you know – always had her plans.

Jo Has she? And what happened about them? Did they work out?

Anna Oh yeah . . . Sometimes.

Jo You trust her.

Anna With my life.

Jo Yeah? Well, supposing I said I don't reckon her plans include us –

Anna That's bullshit, Jo.

Jo Well, we'll see, won't we?

Daniel *walks across, a bulging carrier bag of shoes half hidden under his coat.*

Jo Would you look at . . .

Anna Naughty bugger!

They look at each other. A man in a suit and tie steps into **Daniel***'s path.*

Jo   Shit!

Anna   Store-D, oh Christ. Hope he don't think it was us.

The **Store Detective** *takes* **Daniel***'s carrier bag. Shoes cascade on to the floor.*

Blackout.

Act Two

Scene One

Hayley *is spraying a huge red heart on the back wall.* **Jo** *and* **Lauren** *are acting as lookouts.*

Jo I never would've believed it, if I hadn't been there.

Lauren I thought he was so . . . so straight, you know?

Hayley Yeah, well, you don't know him as well as I do. Even though you'd like to.

Jo Give me Marty any day.

Hayley Who you kidding? Not even yourself, Josephine.

Jo At least my Marty isn't a tea-leaf. Yeah, I know that sounds really hypocritical, but it isn't really.

Lauren It isn't when you think about it. I mean, we nick stuff because we can't afford to buy everything we need – clothes and stuff. Policemen get paid a lot of money, it's not the same.

Jo He should be setting an example. It's as bad as the politicians always screwing around. It's worse because he's nicking other people for doing something he does himself.

Lauren I can't respect Daniel any more.

Jo Still fancy him like hell though, eh?

Lauren *smiles.*

Hayley Just shows he's human like the rest of us.

Lauren He'll have to stop looking down his nose at us.

Hayley There's no difference between him and us now.

Jo So what did he want all those shoes for anyway? Mostly women's and mostly left ones at that. Well? Come on, Hayley, 'she who knows all Danny's innermost secrets'.

Lauren   He's probably some kind of pervert? Is he, Hayley?

Hayley   Does it matter? Does it bother you?

Lauren   No, but I'd like to know –

Jo   The night you gave him a lift home –

Lauren   In a stolen car –

Jo   Did he invite you in? Did you get to see inside his place?

Hayley   He invited me for a coffee and it was really bad because it was the one night I couldn't stop –

Jo   Why?

Hayley   I promised we'd get together one night soon. He seemed really disappointed. Dad was home and you know what he gets like if I stop out –

Jo   Did you get to see inside Danny's place?

Lauren   From the doorstep?

Hayley   It's really tasteful and stylish –

Lauren   And full of ladies' shoes?

Hayley   I'll have a proper look when I go round.

Jo   When's this going to be?

Hayley   Next week maybe. I want to keep things cool for a bit, don't want him to think he's the only one that matters. He's big-headed enough as it is. The way he looks at you with that cruel, teasing smile. He thinks he's God's gift . . . and the really sickening thing is that he is.

Jo   Best bit of crumpet in this tip of a town.

Lauren   What about Marty?

Jo   Well, at least I get to fuck Marty.

Lauren   So do I.

Jo Not recently.

Lauren No?

Jo Shit! You're joking, Lauren. You better be.

She pulls her knife from her pocket. **Lauren** *jumps back.*

You are joking, aren't you?

Lauren Course I am, Jo. I wouldn't piss you around.

Jo *relaxes again.*

Jo But who gets to fuck Daniel? That's what I want to know.

Lauren Probably some really snobby, rich bitch who's got everything.

Jo That's life.

Hayley It needn't be that way.

Lauren Like to see you do something about it. You're all talk, Hay, how we're all going to be rich and living a jet-set lifestyle, but when's it going to happen?

Hayley Soon, Lauren, soon.

Jo So, you'll give me your mountain bike and Anna your computer, three picks each from your wardrobe . . . and what about a bit of cash just to seal the deal properly?

Hayley The cash is for Bali. If I give it to you you'll both fritter it on clothes and dope and downers. You'll get it for your plane tickets soon enough now. Just think of it as a kind of savings account. A quarter of it's your money, Jo, and it'll soon be enough for a one way to Bali. I shouldn't be having to bribe you and Anna anyway, you both love him too.

Jo There're limits.

Hayley Not to me.

Lauren Hayley's a romantic.

Jo   Going soft. If we take the rap for the shoes, we might get a fine. I'm not selling that bike, that's not fair.

Hayley   I expect Danny's got some money. He can take care of it.

Jo   He'd better, I mean, if we're going to do this for him, we expect something in return. What else are we ever going to get from that guy? A cruel smile and a thank you?

Lauren   He told me he isn't going to smile any more. He hates smiling.

Hayley   He what? When?

Jo   God, I'm late for my kick-boxing.

Lauren   I'm going too. Jo's going to start teaching me.

Hayley   How to get your teeth knocked down your throat?

Lauren   You've just got to be ready for anything these days. It's a jungle, right?

Jo   You ought to come, it's really vicious, you'd love it.

Hayley   No, I've other plans for this afternoon.

Lauren   School?

Hayley   Oooh yeah. No, I've a deal to do.

Lauren   Hope it's a profitable one.

Hayley   Remember Bali's only a month away.

Lauren   Can't wait.

Jo   See you, Hay.

Exit **Jo** *and* **Lauren**.

Hayley *turns to face the heart on the wall. She starts to kick it with her boot, harder and harder. She pummels it with her fists. She begins to shriek.*

Enter **Glyn**.

Glyn   Hey . . . what the . . .

Glyn *catches hold of* **Hayley**. *She turns and attacks him with some ferocity. She knocks him down and breaks away. She picks up the spray-can and writes on the wall while he is getting up. She writes 'Pig Lover' across the heart.* **Glyn** *stands up and grabs her wrist making her drop the can. She lets him handcuff her and lead her off.*

Front of stage. **Glyn** *takes the handcuffs off* **Hayley**.

Glyn   Whittaker, Hayley. Again.

Hayley   I haven't been nicked before.

Glyn   More nearlys and almosts than I care to remember. Turn out your pockets.

She does so.

Hayley   Criminal damage? It was only some shitty wall.

Glyn *lays out paper and an ink-pad on the desk. He starts to fingerprint* **Hayley**.

Glyn   How old are you? Fifteen? Sixteen? Got to make some big decisions soon.

Hayley   About what I'm going to do with my life?

Glyn   That's right. Relax your hand.

Hayley   I've got it all mapped out.

Glyn   That so? Well, you don't want to get yourself a criminal record to go wrecking all your dreams now, do you?

Hayley   I've only two dreams, and I'm pretty near to achieving them both now.

Glyn   And the other hand. So what might they be?

Hayley   Travel . . . and romance.

Glyn   Sounds pretty good to me. So you've a boyfriend, have you?

Hayley   What's it to you?

Glyn   What do you think he'd do if he knew you'd been arrested for vandalism?

Hayley   I think he'd smile.

Back of stage.

Daniel *is leaning on the railings looking out to sea. He sees* **Lauren** *and* **Jo** *approaching and exits.*

Front of stage.

Glyn   Come on, Hayley, we'll put you in a cell while we're contacting your parents.

Hayley   Is Sergeant McClune in today? You haven't locked him up have you? Can I see him? Can I now?

Glyn   Why? Won't I do?

Hayley   You what?

Glyn   Doesn't matter. Look, he's not here –

Hayley   Well, call him. Tell him I want to see him.

Exit **Glyn** *and* **Hayley**.

Jo *sits down at the arcade machine.* **Lauren** *looks on.*

Enter **Glyn** *and* **Daniel** *with darts. They begin to play darts.*

Glyn   I couldn't believe it. What ever possessed you? You've buggered up your chance of that job in Gibraltar, and screwed your promotion prospects here for several centuries at least.

Daniel   Life's so dull. You have to take risks.

His darts miss the dartboard.

If there was a bridge and a tightrope which would you take?

Glyn   I wouldn't have got myself suspended.

Daniel   That tightrope every time. If you're facing someone with a knife do you back off or confront them? Why do this job? Could get more money sitting behind a desk. But where else could you get the chills and thrills? I need an adrenalin rush every day – don't you? If nothing's going to happen, if the day doesn't involve any excitement, you have to make some. I can't risk any more warnings for speeding and we still only get the chance of a foot-through-the-floor chase about once a week. It makes me feel like hiring some high-performance cars and leaving them unlocked all around the town.

Glyn   Every time the speedo shoots past ninety, or some psycho's hand moves for their pocket, I think of Gemma and realise how much I want to be there to see her grow up. Find yourself a kind, sexy woman, settle down and have a kid, that's my advice to you.

Daniel   I don't seem to have your luck with the ladies . . .

Glyn *shakes his head, grinning.*

Daniel   Maybe in Gibraltar, some gorgeous señorita, who knows? The chief's already faxed my references to the police there, thank God.

Glyn   But he'll have to let them know about what has happened. It's tough that the shop want charges brought, but there it is, it was a stupid thing to do. And what do you happen to want a whole bag of ladies' shoes for anyway if you don't mind me asking?

Daniel   I don't mind you asking. But I like to keep you guessing, all of you sitting in the mess or the rest room talking about me, speculating about my private life, linking me to anyone and everyone I've ever smiled at.

Glyn   Well, you don't have a lot to smile about at the moment, do you? Was it stress of work, pressure, I mean, do you think?

Daniel   If I don't get this job in Gibraltar, I don't know what I'm going to do! Life here's killing me. Glyn, what should I do?

Glyn   Go and make yourself a strong cup of coffee.

Daniel   If I stay here the trap will close on me. I can't smile here! Every time I do it gets me into trouble. I need to get that job, Glyn.

Front of stage left.

Hayley *jumps up and down on the bed. She kicks the wall, yells and screams.*

Glyn   Jesus. It's that girl. Whittaker, Hayley.

Daniel   Someone ought to go in there and smother her.

Hayley   Daniel! Daniel! I want Daniel! Now!

Glyn   She wants you again. Know her dad, did you say? Can't contact him or her mum. The school don't want to know, washed their hands of the little bitchess.

Hayley   I want Daniel! I want Daniel!

Daniel *looks uneasy, frightened almost.*

Daniel   I think I'll go and make that coffee. And then clear my locker and go home.

Glyn   I've got the weekend off. We could take my brother-in-law's boat out, do some fishing, eh.

He claps **Daniel** *on the back.* **Hayley** *screams.*

It'll be all right.

Exit **Daniel**.

Back of stage.

Jo *and* **Lauren** *are around the arcade machine.*

Jo   Her dad works away and her mum's a receptionist at the clinic. There'll be nobody there.

Lauren   Unless the police have let her go.

Jo   Why'd she want to make all that racket and get herself arrested? It's just plain stupid.

Lauren   Perhaps Daniel's stuck in a cell and she's hoping that she'll get put in the same one.

Jo   Could be fun. I'm worried for Hayley. I mean, she's been doing some reckless things. If she got fined for criminal damage or something she'd have to take the money out of the Bali fund. I really doubt whether we'd ever see any of that money, cash we've risked it all for.

Lauren   It doesn't seem right though, I mean, she's one of us.

Jo *takes a jemmy from inside her jacket.*

Jo   There's no way she'll know it was us.

Lauren   Until we send her a postcard from Bali.

Jo   Let's go, they won't keep her down the nick for ever.

Exit **Lauren** *and* **Jo**.

Front of stage.

Hayley *is sitting on the bed, head in hands.*

Enter **Daniel**.

Hayley *revives instantly.*

Hayley   Took your time. I've been shouting myself hoarse.

Daniel *keeps away from her, he looks around almost as if it is he who is trapped in the cell, not* **Hayley**.

Hayley   How are you?

Daniel   OK.

Hayley   Did they tell you what I'm banged up for?

Daniel   Yeah.

Hayley   I drew a heart on a wall. Really stupid huh?

Daniel   Yeah, almost as stupid as –

Hayley   Trying to nick a load of ladies' shoes. All size eight, left foot only. Can't even sell them at a car-boot. You're a crazy bugger, Danny. You and me both.

Daniel   Now you've seen me will you be quiet and stop giving them all a headache upstairs?

Hayley   Only if you stop here a minute so I can say my piece. Come here and sit down.

Daniel *sits down on the bed beside* **Hayley**. *She takes his hand.*

Hayley   Excuse my inky fingers. Look at yours – nice and clean. They didn't fingerprint you then. Don't treat their own like pieces of shit.

Daniel   If the shop does insist on bringing charges then I'll be fingerprinted and photographed.

Hayley   And it'll get all over the papers, they love anything they can get on a pig. Mind you, it needn't be like that. Danny, did you mean what you said to Lauren about me?

Daniel   I can't remember talking about you with Lauren. I might've said something jokingly. I can't remember.

Hayley   Might you have mentioned something about love?

Daniel   I might've told her I'm in love with you, just to wind her up a bit and keep her guessing.

Hayley   Are you in love with me?

Daniel   I'm not even in love with myself any more. I can't even . . . well, you know . . . enjoy a wank, not with all this worry about changing my job and now this mess with the shoe shop.

Hayley   There's going to be no mess with the shop.

She lies down on the bed.

Lie down beside me.

Daniel   No.

Hayley   Please, Danny.

Daniel   Why?

Hayley   I'd like you to.

Daniel   Someone might look through the flap.

Hayley   But you're in the shit already.

Daniel *lies down beside* **Hayley**.

Hayley   This is really nice. Cosy. And I can talk without being overheard. Listen, sweetheart, here's the pitch. I don't care whether or not you love me, I just want us to be together right, even for only a little while.

Daniel   Like now, you mean?

Hayley   When my mum gets here . . .

Daniel *looks guiltily towards the door.*

Hayley   And they let me out. I can phone Anna straight away. You know Jo was in the shop talking to Anna when you got nicked . . .

Daniel   Very embarrassing. Did they, I mean, were they watching and –

Hayley   Was it Jo and Anna who grassed on you? How can you say that?

She sits up with a horrified expression.

They'd never stab a friend and that's what you are, don't you ever forget it. Friends are precious, Daniel. I know you look down on us, you do, don't deny it. But we care about you, we'd do anything for you. Can you say that about many other people?

Daniel   No . . . and I don't look down on you.

Hayley *strokes* **Daniel**'s *head.*

Hayley   You're a good boy really. Do you like that?

Daniel   Mmm.

Hayley   Enough to give me a smile?

Daniel   I've given up smiling. I've got one of those little arm patches, just stick it on and you can resist the temptation. If you don't smile, people . . . girls don't notice you.

Hayley   I'd still notice you, sweetheart. Anyway, as I was saying, Jo and Anna did notice you nicking the shoes but they didn't see the store detective lurking nearby or they'd have warned you somehow. But listen, they're quite willing to claim they set you up. They put the shoes in your bag for a laugh, cos they don't like pigs. I only have to ring Anna and everything will be OK.

Daniel   But they'll get in trouble.

Hayley   They don't mind. It's well worth it to them.

Daniel   I'm worth it to them?

Hayley   Well . . . I wasn't going to mention this, but I'm bribing Anna with my computer and GameBoy, and giving Jo my mountain bike.

Daniel   What? For saving my neck?

Hayley   You *are* well worth it to me.

Daniel *sits up.*

Daniel   I can't let you do that. Let me think about this. I don't want you doing this. I don't want that kind of help. I've done nothing for you. Well, I suppose I could get you a new mountain bike and a computer, then I wouldn't feel so guilty.

Hayley   No deal.

Daniel What?

Hayley   I don't want the bloody bike and computer, that's why I'm letting those two have them. I want you, Danny.

Daniel Look, I don't know . . .

Hayley   You want me to spell it out? The other evening when I called round you wouldn't let me in. Well, I'm going to call round one evening this week and you are going to let me in. OK? Do you like wine or shall I get some beers?

Daniel And then you'll want to come round the next night and the next.

Hayley   Only because you'll be begging me to. No, this is the deal, you only have to sleep with me the once. Then it's up to you. My dad's away so I don't have to be in at all. I can say I'm staying at Anna's. I've done it loads of times. No one will know, so it's no big deal about me being under age and stuff. And I'm not exactly Miss Innocent, well, you know that and you were there when they searched my room. Why do you always hang around me, why do you come down the arcade when you know I'll be there?

Daniel I don't know.

Hayley   That's a funny way to say yes.

Daniel It's not a yes.

Hayley   Need some time to think?

She goes and sits on the floor.

You told me once that there was something we have in common. Do you remember?

Daniel I can't remember everything I've ever said to you.

Hayley   I can, well, most of it. You said you like doing things just for kicks, just for the hell of it.

Daniel I don't know what I like any more.

Hayley   You like me.

Daniel   I do.

Hayley *rejoins him.*

Hayley   So . . .

Daniel   So.

Hayley   *So?*

Daniel   Yeah.

Hayley   Promise?

Daniel   Like a mint?

Daniel *places the mint between his lips.* **Hayley** *embraces*
Daniel, *taking the mint from his lips with her lips.*

Hayley   I bet you do this trick with all the girls.

Daniel   Oh no, no.

Hayley   Is it special? Just you and me.

Enter **Glyn**.

Daniel *pulls away from* **Hayley**.

Glyn   Whittaker, your mother's here.

He ushers **Hayley** *out.* **Daniel** *sits on the bed.* **Glyn** *comes back
in.*

Glyn   Now I can see why that girl was screaming and
yelling to see you.

Daniel   We're having a mad, passionate fling.

Glyn   Oh my . . .

Daniel   Ah, the kid had got herself in a bit of a state. I
gave her a hug, that's all. Known her since she was this
high.

Glyn   Oh that's right, you know her old man, clay
pigeons, isn't it?

Daniel   I think she's got a bit of a crush on me.

Glyn   Well, if it doesn't work out with the sexy señoritas, and you come back in a few years . . .

Daniel   She'll be living with some layabout and have four kids.

Exit **Daniel** *and* **Glyn**.

Blackout.

Scene Two

Front stage right.

Hayley *sits cutting at her arm with a blade.* **Anna** *comes in.* **Anna** *screams.*

Hayley   Shut up!

Anna   Stop that then.

Hayley   Gone off blood?

Anna   You're sick. No, don't do it any more, I'll . . .

Anna *screams.* **Hayley** *tosses the blade aside.*

Hayley   You're right, I shouldn't get so cut up about it, eh?

Anna   What're we going to do? Did they only take the money?

Hayley   Only? Six hundred quid, Anna.

Anna   And wrecked your room.

Hayley   Shat on my bed.

Anna   Did they?

She hugs **Hayley**.

Oh Hayley.

Hayley   I'd told Mum years ago to get the double-glazing people to fix the window catch . . .

Anna   Did anyone know about the money, apart from us lot?

Hayley   No. No one. Course Mum doesn't know about it. She said we're lucky not to have lost much.

Anna   Did anyone know where you had it stashed?

Hayley   No, but then they trashed the place looking for it.

Anna   You just can't do anything these days. Whatever your dream is, someone comes along and smashes it to bits.

Hayley   It must be someone we know.

Anna   You can't trust anyone these days.

She picks up a notebook.

Oh, they've ripped up your little book.

Hayley *snatches the notebook.*

Hayley   No, I did that. Tore out half the pages, the ones about my plan for us going to Bali. I've only one plan left now.

Hayley *fingers the remaining pages and crams the book into the pocket of her jeans.*

Anna   What's that?

Hayley   My plans for me and Daniel. All the things I'd like to do to him, with him. All the things I will do.

Anna   But what about Bali?

Hayley   It's fucked now.

Anna   We mustn't give up. There must be something we can do. I can't face another year in the shoe shop, or any other government scheme. I had to sit down when you rang and said you'd been robbed of the money. It's like everything I ever wanted has gone. I've wanted to go to

Bali, the Azores or wherever more than . . . anything else
I've ever dreamed of. Because it was real. You were going to
make life worth living.

Hayley   It's still worth living.

Anna   Right now it doesn't feel that way. There must be
something we can do. I know you'll think I'm really stupid
to suggest this, but we could go to the police.

Hayley   I was wondering about that actually.

Anna   But most of the money was . . . well, cash we
nicked.

Hayley   Looks the same as any other money. There's no
way they could identify it.

Anna   Makes it harder for us to get it back though. Are
you sure nothing else's missing?

Hayley   Don't think so.

Anna   Er your computer . . .

Hayley   Is downstairs and so's my GameBoy. The
burglars didn't get that far. So you'll still get your reward for
getting my Danny off the hook.

Anna   I'm going to sell them.

Hayley   What?

Anna   When you give me the computer and GameBoy I'll
sell them and we'll put the money back in the fund for Bali.
Keep it in the bank this time.

Hayley   The GameBoy's clapped and the computer's
prehistoric.

Anna   Thanks very much, you told me they were new.

Hayley   Well . . . I was worried about Danny.

Anna   He's the one who could help us.

Hayley   Maybe.

Hayley *and* **Anna** *move left to sit on the desk.*

Enter **Glyn**.

Glyn   Whittaker, Hayley, again. So what can I do for you?

Anna   She's been burgled. Lost six hundred pounds.

Glyn (*sceptical*)   Oh?

Hayley   Can I see Sergeant McClune?

Glyn   Nope. And you can scream and yell as much as you like, he's taken a few days off.

He hands **Hayley** *a pile of forms.*

If you'd like to fill these in, I'll see what can be done.

Hayley   Shit.

Anna   He doesn't believe us.

Hayley   Or give a toss.

Anna   Nobody does if you're a victim.

Hayley   I'm not a victim, but someone broke into my room, shat on my bed and stole my money.

Glyn   Just fill in the forms.

Hayley   Ring my mum, she'll tell you I'm not lying. I'll write down her number.

Glyn   When was this burglary?

Hayley   This afternoon, while I was down here.

Glyn   Your home from home. So why didn't your mother report this crime to us, or has she already done so . . . ?

Hayley   Mum won't have anything to do with pigs. She's been talking to Lauren's mum. After you went round their place they got two windows broken and their little fir tree painted red. Course, we live in a better area, but Mum says you can't be too careful, especially when Dad's working away. If you send a car, make it a plain one.

Anna   He's not going to send anyone round.

Hayley   If Daniel was here he'd treat it seriously. He'd be concerned.

Anna   He knows people like us have rights.

Hayley   He cares.

Glyn   How well do you know Sergeant McClune?

Hayley   Well enough to know he's not a right old tosser like you.

Glyn   Friend of your dad's, is he? Clay pigeons?

Hayley   He's my lover.

Anna   And mine.

Hayley   He's a fuckin' good lay too.

Anna   He's enormous.

Hayley   Nine inches.

Anna   Bet you don't make half that.

Hayley   Look at his face. He's gone all pinky.

Anna   He almost believes us.

Hayley   Hey, you know we're kidding you around, don't you?

Anna   Not about the burglars though. It's the honest truth.

Hayley   Come on, we're wasting our time here. I'll go see Danny and see if he can think of something.

Exit **Hayley** *and* **Anna**.

Glyn *looks after them for a moment, then picks up the phone.*

Glyn   Hallo, mate, yes it's busy here. Are you? Lucky sod, wish I could. Listen, I've had a couple of your young friends down here again. Yes, Hayley. That's all . . . yes. You don't?

Oh, OK, sorry. Any news about . . . thought you might've come home to find the letter on the mat. Must be any day now though. Talk to you soon.

Back of stage.

A **Man** *is standing facing the railing.* **Hayley**, **Jo**, **Lauren** *and* **Anna** *are grouped around the arcade machine. They are watching him.*

Lauren   He doesn't look rich enough.

Anna   Beggars can't be choosers.

Hayley   He doesn't look like someone I want to kiss.

Anna   Have an extra strong mint. Daniel gave them to me.

Hayley *looks startled, suspicious.* **Anna** *gives* **Hayley** *a mint.*

Jo   Go on, Hay.

Anna   Don't let him get away.

Jo   Trust?

Hayley   Trust.

Hayley *approaches the* **Man**. *He turns. She freezes, suddenly unsure.*

Man   Hallo.

Hayley   Hi ya.

Man   What's the matter?

Hayley   Matter?

Man   Your face is as long as my dick. A smile? A little one did I see?

Hayley   What've I got to smile about?

Man   I could give you something.

Jo *moves closer to* **Hayley** *and the* **Man**.

Hayley   I bet you could too!

Anna   Come on, Hayley. Don't hang about.

Man   So what's your name?

Hayley   Camilla.

Man   Nice. Classy.

Hayley *casts an anxious glance at her friends. They turn away, pretend to be uninvolved.*

Hayley   Thank you.

Anna   Shit, get on with it, or get out of it, Hayley.

Man   Come here often?

Hayley   Only when I'm desperate.

The **Man** *grins.*

Man   Fancy a drink?

Hayley   That's not all I'd fancy.

Man   Yeah.

Hayley   Yeah.

At last she moves in. The **Man** *snatches hold of her and crushes her against him.*

Jo   Now!

The girls move in. The fight is rough. The **Man** *is on top of* **Hayley** *hitting her.* **Lauren** *and* **Anna** *try to pull him off.* **Anna** *screams,* **Hayley** *and* **Lauren** *yell and swear.* **Jo** *unsheaths her knife and moves around looking for a place to stab the* **Man**. *Finally she moves in slashing his hand, breaking his grip on* **Hayley**. *The* **Man** *cries out,* **Lauren**, **Jo** *and* **Anna** *flee.* **Hayley** *stumbles about, hands over her face. Finally she wanders away concussed and dazed, blood running through her hands. The* **Man** *stands up, holding his injured hand.*

Front of stage right.

Daniel, *wearing eyeliner and eyeshadow, carefully sets out a line of women's shoes across the floor. He takes a hammer from beneath the bed and begins to hammer the first shoe in the line until it is wrecked. He hammers the next shoe in the line, and the next.*

There is a knock on the door.

Hayley (*off*)   Danny.

Daniel *does not move. More knocking.*

Hayley   I know you're in there. I could hear you hammering.

Daniel *goes to the door but does not open it.*

Daniel   I can't let you in.

Hayley   You can't break your promise.

Daniel   I have. I am. Leave me alone.

Hayley *pounds on the door.*

Hayley   You promised.

Daniel   Yeah, I'm a right bastard, don't rub it in.

Hayley *thumps the door.*

Hayley   Let me in!

Daniel   I can't.

Hayley   Why not?

Daniel   I don't know. I don't want to see you.

Hayley   Hey, I've something for you.

Hayley *passes a bunch of red roses through the letter box.*

Daniel   You shouldn't have.

Daniel *goes to put the roses in a vase.*

Hayley   Too right I shouldn't. Do you like them?

Daniel   Yes. They're lovely, thank you, Hayley.

Hayley   Will you let me in now?

Daniel   No.

Hayley   You bastard! Tell me why. Tell me or I'll kick the door down. I'll smash your windows, I'll paint your walls red.

Daniel   I just don't need this hassle in my life now.

Hayley   Are you scared of me?

Daniel   No. I'm scared of me.

Hayley   Bullshit . . . well, don't be . . . Come here, sit by the door and let's talk it out.

Daniel *sits down on the floor beside the door.*

Hayley   As far as I can see there can be only two reasons why you won't let me in. Either you find me utterly repulsive or you *are* frightened. Which is it?

Daniel   You're not repulsive, you're very pretty.

Hayley   Pretty, huh? Maybe it's luck you can't see me. My face is all beat up.

Daniel   Been fighting?

Hayley   Are you going to answer my question? Are you frightened?

Daniel   . . . Look, I just don't want to see you.

Hayley   If I could believe that . . .

Daniel   Look . . . I don't feel like . . .

Hayley   Sex?

Daniel   Anything. I'm sorry, Hayley.

Hayley   You will be.

Daniel   I am. I am now.

Hayley   You've messed up my life.

Daniel   Don't be stupid.

Hayley   I can't think of anyone but you.

Daniel   Oh God, Jesus . . .

Hayley   I wake in the night, all I can see is your smile.

Daniel   I've stopped smiling.

Hayley   Look, I want to talk to you. I've been robbed.

Daniel   Call the police.

Hayley   Someone got into our house and took my savings. The pigs didn't want to know.

Daniel   I'll see what I can do in the morning.

Hayley   It doesn't matter. I've still got one plan left. And no one's going to rob me of that.

Daniel   Have you really been burgled?

Hayley   Let me in and I'll tell you about it.

Daniel   Hayley . . .

Hayley   You are scared of me, aren't you?

Daniel   I'm not, it isn't . . . it's only recently you've started to scare me. It's only recently you've started to look at me and not see me, just my body.

Hayley (*laughs*)   What? That's what you think! I've wanted you since I first set eyes on you. Look, if you really can't let me in at least we can sit like this and talk for a while.

Daniel   I don't want to talk.

Hayley   Well, we can just sit and keep each other company, can't we? It's nice just knowing you're near me.

Daniel   These are for you.

He passes a packet of mints through the letter box.

Hayley   Ta.

Hayley's *hand comes through the letter box. It snakes and dances beckoning.* **Daniel** *touches one of her fingers, her hand responds fingers entwining with his and slipping free. Their hands slide together, slide around each other and part, wrists wind around each other in a kind of ballet.*

The phone rings. **Daniel** *pulls free to go to answer it.* **Hayley**'s *hand waits.*

Daniel (*on phone*)   Hi, Glyn.

He looks back at **Hayley**'s *motionless hand.*

Yeah, I got the letter this morning. I've been doing my packing. Yes, I got it! Yeah. I can't quite believe it yet.

Hayley   Danny! Danny!

Daniel   Thanks. Look I've got someone here . . . no, no, nothing like that. I should be so lucky! Yeah, all right, I'll try to pop in. OK, see you tomorrow. Love to Carol and Gemma. Yeah, bye.

Daniel *puts the phone down. He creeps back to the door.* **Hayley**'s *hand hangs heavily, it does not move, she does not detect his approach.* **Daniel** *kneels down, twisting his head beneath* **Hayley**'s *hand, presenting her with his hair to touch, then his ear, finally his mouth, his lips and tongue. He takes her fingers gently in his mouth and works his way across her hand finger by finger. Finally, he gets up and opens the door.*

He leads **Hayley** *by the hand into the room. Her face looks cut and bruised.* **Daniel** *takes her face in his hands and examines it for a moment. He releases her without comment and goes to stand against the back wall, his back to her. She switches the radio on and sways gently.*

Daniel   I'm not going to look at you. Or touch you.

Hayley *goes to* **Daniel**, *her back to his back she rubs cat-like against him.*

Daniel   Hayley, I don't want to . . .

Hayley *turns around and strokes* **Daniel**'s *neck.*

Daniel   We can't . . . I can't . . .

Hayley *strokes* **Daniel***'s back. She burrows her hands under his shirt. He pulls it down and moves her hands back on the outside.*

Lights up back of stage.

Jo *is playing on the arcade machine. The* **Man** *whose hand she slashed walks in. He stands watching her.*

Front of stage.

Hayley *is kissing* **Daniel***'s back. She moves to stroke his legs.*

Daniel (*murmurs*)   No . . . Hayley.

Hayley *slides down to crouch behind him.*

Back of stage.

The **Man** *puts his now bandaged hand on* **Jo***'s shoulder, she turns smiling, probably expecting* **Daniel***. Her expression freezes. The* **Man** *pulls her to her feet by her hair. He drags her from the arcade.*

Hayley *is stroking* **Daniel***'s arse. She slips her hands around front. He gasps, then turns and pulls her to him hard and tight. His hands glide over her body. He backs her up to the bed and topples her on to it, landing heavily on top.*

Back of stage.

The **Man** *pushes* **Jo** *back hard against the pier railing. He lifts her forward and thumps her against the railing again.*

Front of stage.

Daniel *gets up off of* **Hayley***. She reaches out for him. He turns and exits.*

Back of stage.

The **Man** *presses* **Jo** *against the railing, tearing at her clothing, crushing her mouth with his.* **Jo** *struggles and frees one hand. The* **Man** *is fumbling with her clothes. She draws her knife and stabs him in the arse, hard. He falls back. Then comes at her again. She yells.*

Enter **Lauren** *and* **Anna**. *With wild whoops and screams they attack the man.* **Jo** *brandishes her knife.*

Anna   Do it!

Jo *stabs the* **Man** *in the chest. The* **Man** *collapses to his knees, bleeding. The girls scream.*

Exit **Jo**, **Anna** *and* **Lauren**.

Hayley *sits up. She takes out her knife and then her pocket book. She cuts out the remaining pages and scatters them on the floor.*

Hayley *lies face down on the bed.*

Back of stage.

Daniel, *his face set, walks briskly past the* **Man** *without seeing him.*

Man   Hey!

Daniel *sees the* **Man**. *He shrugs and walks on.*

Exit **Daniel**.

Act Three

Scene One

Hayley, **Jo**, **Lauren** *and* **Anna** *are sitting on the floor front, smoking. A cassette player beside them is playing a riot grrrl band* –

Jo   You've got to call him.

Hayley   I will.

Jo   You were with him all night so you're covered but . . .

Hayley   No. I left about seven.

Jo   I thought the deal was –

Hayley   We had a bit of a tiff. I walked out, left him standing there. He called after me, called for me to come back but I kept walking.

Jo   So you've no alibi either.

Lauren   You should have wasted the creep on the pier, Jo. Then he couldn't identify us.

Jo   Oh yeah, get real.

Anna   When do you think it'll be safe to return home?

Jo   I wouldn't, not for a while. Hayley, can you phone Danny right now?

Hayley   . . . Sure.

Jo   Tell him that he has to say that the four of us were at his place till at least eight last night.

Hayley   He may not be very keen –

Lauren   Shit, Hayley, what harm will it do him. He can say we went round to watch a film with him or to get him to do our homework or something.

Jo   He can say anything, the pigs will believe any old bullshit from one of their own. It wouldn't matter if he said he was screwing the four of us. He wouldn't get done.

Hayley   He nearly got done for the shoes.

Jo   But he didn't. Anna lost her job over it.

Anna   He owes us.

Jo   I'm not taking your mountain bike, Hayley, it's Danny who's in my debt. He's the one who must pay.

Lauren   He owes us all.

Jo   Phone him now, here use my card.

Jo *gives* **Hayley** *a phone card.*

Exit **Hayley**.

Lauren   We were so fuckin' stupid. How did we manage to blow three hundred quid each?

Jo   Marty's suit. The ring. Drinks. Dope. Three skirts. Six tops. The Arcade –

Lauren *groans.*

Lauren   We could've nicked half of that stuff. Did you keep any of your receipts?

Jo   We could've got the air tickets and got out of this shit.

Lauren   We'll go to prison, Jo.

Jo   Course we won't. But we'll probably get records. Then they won't take us in Bali or anywhere else. We'll be stuck in this crappy country, with no hope of ever getting a job. We'll have to spend our whole lives steaming and scamming. Or become prossies or something.

Lauren   I don't know why I listened to you, you stupid bitch.

Jo *punches* **Lauren** *in the mouth.* **Lauren** *slaps* **Jo**. **Anna** *comes between them.*

Anna   I don't know how you could do that to Hayley. She was saving that money for all of us.

Jo   You say a word to her, Anna, you're dead meat.

Lauren   I don't think we'd have ever seen that money. I think she was planning to go off somewhere with Daniel.

Jo   Reckon he and her have been plotting something all along.

Lauren   He's going away soon. What's the betting she was going to follow him with all our cash?

Enter **Hayley**.

Jo   Well? What's he say?

Hayley   He's not in.

Jo   Shit.

Lauren   What're we going to do now?

Jo   Phone him again. Try every ten minutes.

Hayley *switches the music off.*

Hayley   Actually . . . he was in. But he was just going out, to buy his flight tickets. He's starting a new job in Gibraltar next month, and he's flying out tomorrow for a couple of weeks' holiday first.

Anna   Lucky sod.

Jo (*quickly*)   When did he tell you this?

Hayley   A minute ago.

Jo   And our alibi?

Hayley   He won't. He said he couldn't do anything else for us. He said goodbye.

Hayley *takes out her notebook.*

Anna   Wish I'd been able to give him a goodbye kiss.

Jo   He can't even say it face to face. That's what we mean to him. He's just a tease, a flirt, he thinks fuck all of us.

Lauren   I bet he's laughing at us.

Hayley   I asked him why he wouldn't sleep with me. He wouldn't give me an answer.

Lauren   He thinks he's too good for us.

Jo   He thinks you're just some bit of trash, Hayley, some old slapper. Fine for a bit of a joke and a bit of a flirt.

Hayley   But not good enough to fuck.

Hayley *kicks the cassette player over. She takes out a pen and writes in her notebook.*

Anna   What're you writing?

Hayley   A new plan.

Jo   So Daniel was just going out was he?

Hayley   Come on, you guys, anyone got some change for a tube of mints?

Exit **Hayley**, **Jo**, **Lauren** *and* **Anna**.

Front of stage.

Enter **Daniel** *and* **Glyn**.

Glyn   I can understand you not wanting a leaving party and all that fuss. You'll be missed though. I expect you'll miss this place too in some ways . . .

Daniel   Yeah.

Glyn   Look, if you'd like to pop round this evening –

Daniel   Sorry I won't be –

Glyn   Just for half an hour or so –

Daniel   I'd like to, but –

Glyn   Please.

Daniel   Sorry –

Glyn   Here.

He pushes a little parcel into **Daniel***'s hand.*

It's nothing really.

Daniel *opens the parcel. It contains a wallet.*

Glyn   Look inside.

Daniel   A lucky sixpence.

Daniel *opens the wallet, pulls out a couple of BT phone cards.*

Glyn   Just a couple of phone cards. You can use them in Gibraltar. I've checked. So you'll remember to call sometimes and let me know how it's going, eh?

Daniel   Thanks, Glyn.

Glyn *tries to hug* **Daniel**.

Glyn   God, it's been like a mad house here today. I bet you're glad you're out of it.

Daniel   Mmmm.

Glyn   You don't seem too excited about the prospect of all that sun, sea, sex . . .

Daniel   It hasn't sunk in yet . . . I suppose.

Glyn   Not having second thoughts or anything?

Daniel   No.

Glyn   God. I wish it was me, leaving this place. Did you hear about what happened last night? Those girls again, I'm sure of that. Stabbed some guy on the pier.

Daniel   Bad?

Glyn   Pretty. He's in intensive, punctured lung. I . . . I didn't want to cause any hold-ups or hassles for you, so I didn't mention your connection with that girl Whittaker.

Daniel   Has she been charged?

Glyn   No, but her name's blowing in the wind. Hers and one or two of her bosom buddies – a girl who came down the nick with her earlier, some story about a burglary, they left without reporting it officially, thank God. I've enough paperwork.

Daniel   It wasn't Hayley.

Glyn   Eh?

Daniel   She was with me last night.

Glyn   About what time . . . ?

Daniel   From sixish.

Glyn   To?

Daniel   She was with me all night.

Daniel *drains his cup and stands it on the desk.*

Glyn   *She was!?*

Daniel   Matter of fact they all were. Hayley, Lauren, Jo and Anna. Must get back and finish my packing. Love to Carol and Gemma, and take care, mate.

Exit **Daniel**.

Glyn *looks after him.*

Front of stage.

The door is open. **Jo** *holds a jemmy and a splintered piece of wood.* **Hayley** *and* **Anna** *sit on the bed.* **Jo** *and* **Lauren** *stand by the door.* **Hayley** *lies down and flops forward to look under the bed. She takes out* **Daniel**'s *box of make-up. She picks a lipstick and eyeshadow compact. She passes the box to* **Anna**. **Anna** *chooses some make-up and throws some to* **Jo** *and* **Lauren**. *The girls make their faces up dramatically, scarlet slashes for lips, dark eye sockets. They begin painting each other's faces. Hearing* **Daniel** *approaching,* **Jo** *moves to stand behind the door.*

Enter **Daniel**.

Daniel *gasps to see the girls in his house. He is holding his passport.*
Jo *kicks him from behind, taking him by surprise. She snatches the*
passport. **Lauren** *knees* **Daniel** *in the stomach.* **Hayley** *waits,*
standing on the bed. **Jo**, **Lauren** *and* **Anna** *take hold of* **Daniel**.
Jo *holds her knife to his throat as they drag him over to the bed where*
Hayley *stands waiting.* **Daniel** *struggles.* **Hayley** *kicks him in*
the head, knees him in the balls. The girls drag the half-conscious
Daniel *across the bed, pinning his arms and legs.* **Lauren** *and* **Jo**
unbutton and pull off his shirt. **Hayley** *pulls down his jeans and*
pants. She straddles and sits astride **Daniel**. **Jo** *holds her knife to his*
throat as **Hayley** *leans forward to kiss him.* **Hayley** *pinches his*
nose to try to make him open his mouth but he manages to buck her off
and scramble off the bed. **Anna** *and* **Lauren** *leap up, grab his legs*
and pull him down on to the floor. The struggle starts over again.
Daniel *is frantic and frightened.* **Jo** *manages again to get her knife to*
his throat, subduing him.

Hayley *brings* **Daniel**'s *make-up over to where the other three girls*
have him pinioned on the floor. The girls smear **Daniel**'s *body with*
handfuls of lipstick, eyeshadow, mascara and blusher, sometimes
shrieking, screaming obscenities or making pig noises, sometimes
murmuring softly and caressing him, as he struggles. **Daniel** *is*
sprawled on his stomach with the girls sitting on him. They stripe his
back and arse with the cosmetics with long sweeping strokes. He looks
like a patchwork quilt.

Hayley *straddles* **Daniel**'s *back, sits astride him. She takes a tube*
of mints from her pocket. The other girls watch with eager anticipation.
Hayley *takes out a mint, wrenches* **Daniel**'s *head up, forces the*
mint into his mouth.

Hayley   I love you, Daniel.

Together the girls leap up and rush out.

Blackout.

Scene Two

Daniel *sits wrapped in a blanket, staring into space. The white-coated* **Doctor** *and* **Glyn** *are with him.*

Glyn   Just tell me who . . . give me the names –

Doctor   Perhaps we should leave him alone for –

Glyn   Who did this to you? Who?

Doctor   It might not be . . . er, quite as it seems . . . this . . . this . . . might be something he initiated, that is to say.

Glyn *glares at the* **Doctor**.

Glyn   He was attacked! My friend was attacked, what are you trying to say, that he was asking for it? That he's in some way responsible? Christ! You're disgusting, you're just . . .

Doctor   Well, until he feels able to tell us what happened, perhaps one shouldn't speculate –

Glyn   Danny, Danny? Is he in shock?

Doctor   Difficult to tell, isn't it?

Glyn   I think we should leave him for a bit . . .

Exit **Glyn** *and the* **Doctor**.

Daniel *picks up the tube of mints from the floor, he takes one out and looks at it.*

Blackout.

Stealing Souls

Stealing Souls was first performed at the Red Room, London, on 5 April 1996. The cast was as follows.

Vince   Tom Marshall
Maria   Raquel Cassidy

Directed by Shabnam Shabazi
Designed by Roswitha Gerlitz
Lighting by John Sharian
Music by Kate Heath

A room in the Flamengo Palace Hotel, Rio de Janeiro, Brazil. Early hours of the morning.

The room is dimly lit by lamps and scented candles. Music plays softly.

Vince Stanier, *a photographer, sits cross-legged and still on the bed.* **Dr Maria Segundo** *stands by the door, holding her medical bag.*

Maria   An emergency, they said.

Vince   Four hours, thirty-six bloody minutes.

Maria   I was expecting something serious.

Vince   I'm in agony.

Maria (*unimpressed*)   Ay.

Vince   Been awake all night with the pain.

Maria   In your tooth?

Vince (*snaps*)   No, in my arse. Look, you really are the dentist, not room service or dial-a-whore?

Maria   I'm a doctor.

Vince *turns off the music.*

Vince   Shit. Dentist, *dentista*! I told them.

Maria   I know about teeth . . .

Vince   I know about cunts, darling, but that doesn't make me a gynaecologist.

Maria   I must be crazy. I must be going completely mad . . . I thought someone was dying up here. A matter of life and death they said.

Vince   No dentist on a Sunday was all they kept telling me, so after ringing the desk every hour on the hour and getting that same old shit, I carefully cradled the receiver against the good side of my jaw . . . (*He demonstrates.*) Took a deep breath and . . . HELP! GOD! JESUS! HELP ME! OH GOD! . . . . shit, that fucking hurt.

Maria   I thought . . . I thought there would be other people here, someone else at least. Perhaps your wife . . .

Vince (*amused*)   . . . Wife.

Maria *turns to go.*

Maria   I'm sorry. I cannot help. See the dentist on Monday.

Vince *gets up.*

Vince   Hey! Wait a minute. You said you knew about teeth.

Maria   Yes . . . and you said . . .

Vince   That I know about cunts, well, I do, and my interest is as strictly professional as yours.

Maria   I'm sorry –

Vince (*sharply*)   About what?

Maria   I shouldn't have come up here.

Vince *blocks the doorway.*

Vince   What're you afraid of?

Maria   I wish to leave.

Vince   Afraid of me?

Maria   I don't know you. You could be . . .

Vince   A rapist?

Maria   Let me go now.

Vince   Is that what you think? You think I'll jump you and rape you? Sure, I do it all the time – pretend I've got toothache to lure a lady doctor up here, then rape her, strangle her, and shut her body in the wardrobe. Go on,

open it up, have a look in there. See how many skeletons
I've got in my cupboard.

He moves away from the door.

Get out! Get out of my fucking room! *Fora! Fora!* I've never
been so fucking insulted!

Maria   You're insulted, ay!

Vince   Do you naturally assume that every man who calls
you out in the middle of the night wants to have his wicked
way with you?

Maria   No, but –

Vince   Take a look at yourself, no offence, Doctor, but
you're hardly a vision of love's young dream. Oh shit – I'm
always ratty at this time in the morning, even when I
haven't had a rough night. Let's start again, shall we? Oh,
come on . . . still scared, Doctor?

Maria   I think it is you who is scared.

Vince *laughs, then holds his jaw.*

Maria   Ah, you're not pretending.

Vince   Huh?

Maria   You said you pretend to have toothache, just to
. . . get a woman to come up here.

Vince   Shit, man, don't people in this bloody country ever
listen!

Maria *opens her bag.* **Vince** *buttons up his shirt, checks his fly,
flattens his hair, squeezes a little toothpaste from a tube.*

Maria   What're you doing, Mr . . .

Vince   Vince Stanier. Eating toothpaste.

Maria   Eating it?

Vince   To stop my breath killing you at ten paces.

Maria   You don't like Brazilian cuisine, Mr Stanier?

Vince   Love it, when I'm able to eat it. Are you hungry? There's a gorgeous dish of cold rice and orange going to waste here.

He brings the dish to **Maria**.

Vince   Smells good, eh?

Maria   Mmmm.

Vince   Go on, tuck in.

Maria   When I've seen to that tooth maybe.

Vince   Eat it now. The sight of my suppurating molar will spoil your appetite.

Maria *picks at the food.*

Maria   Is this your first visit to Brazil, Mr Stanier?

Vince   Rio is my home from home. I come here when I need to be surprised, excited, stimulated, when I need to remind myself that I'm alive . . . when I can afford it. This is where I find my inspiration. Where I felt inspiration for the first time, in fact.

Maria   You write then? Or paint?

Vince   No, I . . . I'm sorry, I can't watch a woman eat.

Maria   I beg your . . .

Vince   I can't look at a woman while she's eating, it touches me.

Maria   Ay.

Vince   When a woman raises an item of food to her mouth, I feel kinda awkward about being there and seeing her at that moment. It's like watching her undressing, or in the bath. Eating, she gives something of her true self away. It's a moment of intense revelation.

Maria   Really?

She continues to eat.

Vince   No – I can't stand it!

Maria   Shall I stop?

Vince   Continue, please. Don't let me spoil your meal.
Take no notice of me.

*He turns away, but keeps taking sly glances at her when he thinks she's
not looking.*

Why is it Brazilian women eat so little?

Maria   Do we?

Vince   I had this girlfriend . . .

Maria *puts her fork down.*

Vince   A Brazilian girlfriend – ate like a bird . . . no, like a
butterfly. I never understood why she didn't waste away.
She was very beautiful, though she had rather large teeth.

Maria *pushes the dish away.*

Vince   Perhaps I'm unkind to her memory. Maybe I only
remember her teeth as large as all I have left are the scars
they made.

Maria   Oh my . . . this girl . . . may I ask . . . where did
she bite you?

Vince   Usually in bed, sometimes in the car.

Maria   And why –

Vince   Do you think she was sick, Doctor?

Maria   Do you?

Vince   Biting me used to quieten her, seemed to give her
some kind of comfort – Like a child suckling at its mother's
breast, I don't know.

Maria   Perhaps there was little else to comfort her in her
life. Where did –

Vince   Right in the crook of my arm. Look, see there and there? Blood fascinated her. Sounds morbid, but she wasn't. If I'd cut myself shaving she'd want to touch and sniff and taste. She'd press her cheek to mine and smear the few droplets across her own face. I see her now laughing, blood below her high cheekbones, blood on her big teeth.

Maria   Did you love her very much?

Vince   I didn't know it 'til she was gone. Rather, I had gone, home to England.

Maria   Shall I look at that tooth now? Mr Stanier? What, what is it?

Vince   Nothing. Ghosts of the past, that's all.

Maria   They visit me too sometimes.

Vince   But yours are probably friendly ghosts, Doctor.

Maria   No, not friendly . . . lonely ghosts maybe. Now don't be nervous, I'll just look to begin with, nothing else.

Vince   You won't be able to see anything.

Maria   . . . Unless you let me try. Sit under the light, please.

Maria *takes a mirror and a probe from her bag.*

Vince   Not that meat hook! Is it sterilised? Unless you sterilise it first, you're not getting that anywhere near my gob.

Maria   You're impossible! I'm wasting my time!

Vince   I better show you which tooth . . .

Vince *opens his mouth.*

Maria   It is this tooth, yes? This one?

Vince   Ow! Yeah . . . don't touch it.

Maria   The gum's very swollen. Does it hurt . . .

Vince   Ow! Shit . . .

Maria   And here?

Vince   Ahhh!

Maria   Here?

Vince *leaps up.*

Maria   Hurt a lot, huh?

Vince   No shit.

Maria   You've an abscess, a large one. You'll have to see the dentist on Monday.

Vince   Monday! Can't you give me some painkillers or something?

Maria   Some aspirins, certainly.

Vince   I'm already taking those by the dozen. Something stronger.

Maria   Very well. I'll write you a prescription. The chemist won't be open until Monday though.

Vince   Fucking Monday! I'll have to go down into the town as soon as it gets light, see if I can find anyone down a back street who can pull a tooth.

Maria   And you'll get yourself hit over the head and wake up with your money gone and all your teeth pulled.

Vince   Well, what else can you suggest?

Maria   I suppose I could try to take the tooth out for you and lance that abscess.

Vince   'Try'? Would it be very difficult?

Maria   Not really.

Vince   What do you usually do – as a doctor?

Maria   Everything. From birth to . . . death.

Vince   Have you taken a tooth out before?

Maria   It doesn't take long. Usually it's quite easy.

Vince   Right then.

Maria   But with an abscess . . .

Vince   What?

Maria *lays out her instruments.*

Maria   Have you a couple of clean cups and a large bowl?

Vince   Cups, yeah, and a bowl.

Maria   For the blood.

Vince   Wait . . . How much is this going to cost?

Maria   It depends.

Vince   On?

Maria   How long it takes.

Vince   The longer it takes the more I owe you, eh?

Maria   That's right.

Vince   You'll take as long as you can then, won't you?
Wait . . . How about if I pay you in reverse?

He fetches the cups and bowls.

Maria   I don't understand.

Vince   I'll pay you more if you do it quickly, less if you
take a long time. Traveller's cheques or rayale?

Maria   Cash would be best.

Vince   Like the whores and the models. Hope I've enough
left.

Maria   Models?

Vince   Photographic.

Maria   Ah.

Vince   What do you mean 'ah'? It's all quite respectable
. . . these days.

Maria   I think . . . you'd better instead go to the dentist on
Monday.

Vince   Don't you think you can do it, after all?

Maria   I can do it, but you'll make too much fuss, such a
great commotion. A dentist would be able to give you a
proper anaesthetic.

Vince   Whisky! I've a bottle somewhere.

Maria   I could rub it around the tooth. It might numb it a
little.

Vince   Fuck that. I'm gonna finish the bottle.

Maria   Ay, ay, ay, I don't think you should . . .

Vince   You sound like my mother.

He fetches the bottle and glasses.

Have one yourself, Doctor.

Maria   No thank you.

Vince   You've quite a tremble there.

Maria   Perhaps it is a little cold in here.

Vince   Bollocks. Alright, I'll close the window, shall I?
You're more nervous than I am. Well, don't be, I can
virtually guarantee it will hurt me more than it does you.
Just half a glass, I'm superstitious about drinking alone.

He lifts his glass.

See, no shake? The stoicism of the Englishman abroad.
Cheers.

Maria *lifts her glass.*

Maria (*solemnly*)   Here's looking at you, kid.

Vince *splutters whisky everywhere, holds his jaw.*

Maria   Are you laughing?

Vince   It used to a little joke between Ines and me.

Maria   Oh.

Maria *gulps her whisky and chokes.*

Vince   Ines who preferred to drink blood.

Maria   Was *Casablanca* her favourite too?

Vince   We watched it on telly when she was still at school and knew hardly any English.

Maria   A long time ago?

Vince   My first trip to Brazil. Nineteen, maybe twenty years ago. I've some pictures of her somewhere.

He rummages among his things, takes out some photos.

This is some of my work – various shoots for magazines and brochures. Assorted views mainly. Looking down from the Corcovado Christ at sunset, the view from Sugar Loaf in spring. The carnival, the festival of Jesus of Seafarers. Ah . . .

Maria   Is this her?

Vince   Ines? No that's another girl . . . er . . . Clara. There's some more of Clara . . .

He looks at each photo, then passes them to **Maria***, who is becoming restless.*

Some more girls.

Maria   Mainly you photograph girls?

Vince   Nice work if you can get it.

Maria   For girlie magazines? British girlie magazines?

Vince   American and German ones more often. The Germans like their Brazilian women to be real Amazonians . . .

Maria   Was Ines . . .

Vince   God, no. She was small, quiet. Here she is, in a favourite pose.

Maria   Hers or yours? She looks very young.

Vince   She was fourteen. I put her on a pedestal. Here she is again.

Maria   The way she's sitting . . . looking over her shoulder, twisting a strand of hair around her finger . . .

She mimics the pose. **Vince** *snatches up his camera, photographs her.*

Hey! Is there film in there?

Vince   That's good, you're a natural. Try this one. Turn the chair around.

Maria *takes up the pose.*

Maria   Like this?

Vince   Yeah, but you're too tense. You're all angles where, look, she's smoothly flowing. No harsh lines. See how her legs and toes point. That's better, much better. But you're still hunching your shoulders. Deep breaths, relax. You've a natural poise and grace but you're way too tense. You should go to dance classes or aerobics to loosen yourself up a bit.

He picks up his camera again.

Smile. Open mouth – how're your teeth? Just a little. OK. But don't clench your jaw, I'm the one with the toothache. Nice and relaxed.

He moves around her with the camera.

Try looking down, right down here. Now glance up at the camera. Terrific.

Maria   *Is there film in the camera?!*

Vince   I've some more of Ines. Special ones. I don't usually show people these.

He hands the photos to **Maria**. *He watches over her shoulder as she studies them.*

Beautiful, aren't they?

Maria   She looks sad . . . sad and scared.

Vince   She's smiling in every one.

Maria   Her eyes are not smiling. When you sold these pictures . . .

Vince   I didn't. They were just for me.

Maria   Did she know that?

Vince   I expect I made her a few promises, I mean, she could've been a top model if these had landed on the right desk.

Maria   And escaped from her life of poverty.

Vince   Yes, her family was poor. But they were close to each other and happy. She didn't have any great ambitions to go jetting off somewhere, so I don't feel bad about keeping these just for myself.

Maria   So you think she was content, huh?

Vince   She was happy-go-lucky, if rather intense.

He puts the photos away.

I taught her to read English and she read every book and magazine in the place. She was that clever.

Maria   Her parents knew she came to you?

Vince   Her father introduced us at a party. He didn't know I'd arranged to see her the following day, and he never found us out. She told him she'd found a lonely old spinster to teach her English.

Maria   A respectable girl wouldn't have let herself be photographed like this. She'd have been in school or studying for her exams.

Vince   She was a respectable girl.

Maria   Before or after m⸺ng you?

Vince   She still is ⸺. A few years ago, I saw a picture of her in ⸺ have the cutting in my wallet. It's ⸺

Maria ⸺

Vince   I c⸺med to say.

Maria (reading⸺ on the beach at Leblon is still to ⸺ed, but is thought to be that of missing n⸺ verde –'

Vince snatches the p⸺

Vince (softly)   Ines.

Maria   'Foul play is not suspected . . .'

Vince   She loved life. She devoured it. She was devout, she never missed mass. A good girl, a good family. She was, she was . . .

Vince sobs. **Maria** stands up, moves away from him.

Maria   Mr Stanier . . .

She goes back to him.

Vincent, querida amigo, Vincent . . .

Vince looks up, startled.

Maria   Querida amigo, Vincent, nao foi por querer que o magoei . . . I didn't hurt you on purpose.

Maria picks up and examines the camera.

Vince   A stealer of souls, according to a superstition in these parts.

Maria   I don't think you can steal someone's soul.

Vince   Suppose that they gave it to you?

Maria   Gave you their soul? What would you do with it?

Vince   Cherish it.

Maria   Betray it.

Vince   No.

He pulls a suitcase from under the bed.

This is where I keep her.

Maria   Her?

Vince   Her memory.

He pulls a beautiful emerald-green dress from the case.

Vince   She wanted to have this. I said I needed it for other girls. Actually, I won't let anyone else try it on, but I do use it to tempt them: 'If you're as good as Ines you can have this,' I say. They try but of course they don't come close. When I'm in a lonely hotel room, in a lonely city at a lonely hour of the morning, I take it out, unfold it and shake out the creases. If you'd like one of the other dresses I'll give it to you.

Maria   If I pull your tooth? You said you could pay.

Vince (*snaps*)   Of course I'll bloody pay you! I was just going to make you a present, that's all.

Maria   Why? You haven't let me take the tooth out yet. I wonder if you are going to. I wonder if you're only wasting my time.

She checks her watch.

Look how long you've kept me here.

Vince   Do you have other calls to make? Go then. Am I delaying you while someone lies dying?

Maria   I've no more calls tonight. If there's an emergency, the clinic will bleep me.

Vince   Haven't you been working a long day, don't you yearn to go home to your bed?

Maria   I'm a night owl, but I'll go now if you don't need me.

Vince   I didn't say that.

Maria *looks at the green dress, then sees* **Vince** *is looking at her.*

Maria   It is beautiful.

Vince   Try it. For you I'll make an exception. Go on, try it.

Maria   For whose benefit?

Vince   You can change in the bathroom if you're shy, Doctor . . . You never did tell me your name?

Maria   Dr Segundo.

Vince   First name?

Maria   Maria.

Vince   There's a comb in the bathroom, perhaps you could put your hair up.

Maria   Like Ines in the photos? . . . OK.

Vince   OK? Great.

Maria   But I shall take your tooth out first.

Vince   The green goes with your eyes.

Maria *puts a towel over* **Vince**, *hands him the bowl.*

Maria   Open.

She inserts the probe and pliers in his mouth. Suddenly he yells, closes his mouth on her hand, and knocks her away from him. She stands looking intently at her hand.

Vince   Fuck it! Oh shit.

He looks in the mirror.

The bastard's still there and it's killing me now. You've mangled the gum and barely wobbled the tooth. Are you sure you know what you're doing? You really have done this before, haven't you? I can't endure any more of this, I'll be climbing the fucking wall in a minute.

Maria (*brightly*)   Ready for another tug?

Vince   No way.

Maria   One more and then no problem . . . unless . . .

Vince   . . . It still won't budge, then worse than agony.

Maria   You make too much fuss, you're impossible. I'll get it this time. I'll brace myself against the chair.

Vince   Wish I shared your confidence.

Maria   I might have to cut the gum, just a little . . .

Vince   More whisky! Lots more. And aspirin.

Vince *takes some aspirins with a gulp of whisky. He swigs some more straight from the bottle.*

Maria (*tutting*)   Living dangerously, Mr Stanier.

Vince   I need something stronger. Haven't you anything in that little black bag of yours, doctor?

Maria   Nothing suitable.

Vince   Maybe I can go out and get something.

Maria   The chemist doesn't open until Monday.

Vince   I know some people, from the *favelas*, hang about on the beach at night.

Maria   You'll get yourself murdered.

Vince   Probably be lot less painful . . .

Maria   So much fuss! You're completely crazy. Go then, go and get yourself killed!

She opens her case.

Or maybe . . . maybe I could give you something. A little morphine maybe.

Vince   Now you're talking.

Maria   This is not good. I could get into trouble and maybe . . .

She fills the syringe.

Maybe you're also afraid of needles.

Vince   Fortunately not.

He rolls up his sleeve, but does not look as she injects him. She remains looking at the tiny smear of blood on his arm as if mesmerised.

Is it all right? You put it in the right place, didn't you? You hit the vein?

Maria   No problem.

Vince   I feel kinda like suddenly something's coming back to me.

Maria   Tell me when it starts to hit the pain, Vince.

Vince   Vince? Oh yeah, I did tell you . . . This is good shit.

Vince *laughs.*

Maria   What is it?

Vince   The Jardim Botánico. Walking hand in hand along the palm-lined avenue. Every time I turned to look at your face you were smiling. Smiling and showing off your big white teeth. Your hand in mine was so warm. Those water lilies, what were they called?

Maria (*softly*)   Victoria regia.

Vince   Their leaves as big as a room. I asked you to stand on one, to step from the paved edge of the pond on to the huge flat leaf, so you'd look like a water nymph . . .

Maria   Ay.

Vince   The stems were quite thick, the leaf was strong.
You didn't believe it was safe though. You thought you'd be
tipped in the water. I wanted that picture, you in your deep-
emerald dress in the middle of the leaf, a few drops of
trapped water sparkling around your feet like diamonds. My
nymph of the fountain.

Maria   Yes.

Vince   I put the camera strap over your head, let you look
through the viewfinder, altered the focus for you so you
could see what a perfect, enchanted place I'd chosen to be
graced by your beauty. Still you were wary, but I told you
that you were a dragonfly able to alight on the leaf without
even causing it to dip a little or ripple the water.

So as delicately as a ballerina you stepped from the firm
rock on to the floating leaf – and it tipped you straight in the
water. To my eternal regret I forgot to press the shutter. If
I'd photographed that moment, I'd have trapped your spirit,
stolen your soul.

You could've drowned, darling, while I stood there
laughing. But you crawled from the water, dragonfly no
longer, instead a slimy, green amphibian. Quite a crowd
was gathering, having heard the splash. A loud fat woman
ran up to you shouting some words I didn't understand,
scolding in a motherly kind of way. You pushed her away,
you met my eyes and you grinned. You threw back your
head and laughed, laughed as if you were laughing at me.
Your teeth looked huge, predatory, devouring. I ran to
embrace you to stop the hysteria, or whatever it was that
was making you laugh like you'd lost all possession of your
senses. I tried to hug you – I hugged air. Your footsteps
pounded up the avenue of palms. I sprinted after you,
expecting the sodden dress dragging around your legs to trip
you, but you reached the Rua and I lost you amidst the
traffic. Ines!

Maria *leaves the room with the green dress.*

Vince   Wait! Ines! *Nao foi por querer que o magoei!* Ines, I
didn't mean to hurt you.

*He throws all the dresses out of the case, rummages in the bottom, takes
out an English/Portuguese dictionary. He unfolds the newspaper
cutting, then flicks through the dictionary.*

Cas . . . Casamento – wedding. *Feliz* – happy. *Fotografia*, yeah.
Photograph of the . . . happy . . . occasion? . . . couple?
Casamento – wedding of Ines Verde and . . .

Maria *comes in wearing the green dress.*

Vince   Dr Felipe Segundo. Dr Segundo. Death.

He flicks through the dictionary.

Vince   *Mort.*

He checks the article for the word.

No. Try drowned, drowning. No mention of death or
drowning. Body? Washed up? Accident? Suicide?

He continues to flick through the dictionary. He looks up, sees **Maria**.

There's nothing here about her drowning and being washed
up on Leblon beach. You lied, she isn't dead.

Maria   You stole her soul, how could she live?

Vince   I'm going crazy or else it's the morphine . . .
You're not her come back, you can't be . . . And you're not
having my darling's dress, it's all I have left of her.

Maria   You have the photos.

Vince   I can't take them to bed at night.

Maria   You have your scars.

Vince   Everyone has those.

Maria   That dress is mine. I gave you my soul for it.

Vince *grabs hold of her.*

Maria   Have I changed so much?

Maria *laughs, throwing her head back.*

Vince   Your teeth, Ines . . .

Maria   I had them fixed.

Maria *sits* **Vince** *down on the bed, rolls his sleeve up to the elbow. She turns the lamp low and the soft music back on, before lifting the crook of his arm to her teeth.*

Blackout.

Sunspots

Sunspots was first performed at the Red Room, on 21 May 1996. The cast was as follows:

Pola	Raquel Cassidy
Sam	Robert Calvert
Aimee	Sarah Theresa Belcher
Jake	Jake Nightingale

Directed by Lisa Goldman
Designed by Annabel Shapiro
Lighting by David Plater
Sound by Dave Sharp
Music by John Evans
Assistant Director Bernie Moran

Act One

Scene One

Hastings Station. Afternoon. Spring. Sounds of a train pulling in.

Pola *(late twenties, in Kangol beret, fluorescent T-shirt, blue John Lennon shades) is spraying her tag 'SISS' on a wall, below a sign saying 'Welcome to Hastings'.*

An announcement crackles over a speaker. **Pola** *mimes the words – she obviously knows all the announcements by heart.*

Announcement   Hastings, this is Hastings. The train now on Platform Two terminates here. All change please on Platform Two. All change please.

Enter **Aimee** *and* **Sam** *with suitcases. (***Sam**, *smart but unfashionable, serious-looking, forties;* **Aimee**, *mid-twenties, in jeans and jacket, and a big crystal pendant.)*

Sam   I can't get over it.

Aimee *looks about her.*

Sam   How much did they charge for you for that sandwich?

Aimee *spots* **Pola** *tagging. Worried,* **Aimee** *tries to keep* **Sam** *from noticing.*

Aimee   I know, it was outrageous –

Sam *(interrupting)*   So where is she then? Give me some idea of what I'm supposed to be looking for? Is she the sort of person who's usually early or late?

He spots **Pola**.

(Outraged.)   Aimee . . . look at that. In broad daylight. The nerve of him! And no one's doing anything . . .

He approaches **Pola**, **Aimee** *following, not really knowing what to do.*

Hey! Hey, you there, Michelangelo!

Pola *turns to see* **Aimee** *and* **Sam**.

Pola   Aimee!

Pola *pockets the can, hugs* **Aimee**.

Aimee   And this is Sam.

Pola   Yes . . .

Pola *and* **Sam** *stare at each other.*

I imagine it is. Congratulations, Sam.

Sam   And this . . . this . . . what you're doing here . . .

Pola   Tagging.

Sam   Well, doesn't anyone stop you?

Pola   It's my wall.

Sam   Your . . . ?

Pola   It's a special wall provided for the local artists. Nice idea, eh?

Sam   How very . . . enlightened . . . of British Rail or whoever owns all of this these days.

Aimee   I'm sorry our train was a bit late . . .

Sam   Aren't they always?

Aimee   . . . Have you been waiting long?

Pola *checks where her watch would be if she had one.*

Pola   Only about twelve months.

Aimee   I'm glad you could change your plans and see us . . . before we go.

Sam   Guess how much Aimee had to pay for a sandwich on the train? Go on, guess.

Pola   Ten quid.

Sam   Well, no —

Pola   Higher or lower?

Aimee   It was two ninety-nine, for a packet of two.

Pola   You should've waited for happy hour.

Sam   Really? I'd no idea there was such thing as a happy hour on Network SouthCentral, or that it included sandwiches.

Pola   Well, there you go then. You learn something every day . . . or so they say.

Sam   Isn't it cold? I can't wait to get to warmer climes, where the beaches are sun-drenched as opposed to just plain drenched.

Pola   I take it you didn't bring your cossie and your factor seven, Sam?

Aimee   Did you go swimming in the summer?

Pola   Check out my tags in waterproof ink on every buoy between here and Bexhill.

Sam   Don't you worry about the sea being polluted?

Pola   I expect you'll have to in Cyprus.

Pause.

Sam   I'll have to find a call box in a minute, see if anything's transpired at the meeting . . .

Aimee   Sam, I thought when you promised to leave the mobile at home —

Sam   Only one quick call, Aimee. Pola, I was saying to Aimee on the way down, I can't imagine why anyone should still want to take their holiday at an English seaside resort. They always seem such shabby, shoddy places, with precious little to offer in the way of culture and entertainment, unless you enjoy second-rate, tawdry little comedians and embarrassingly talentless talent shows.

Aimee   Sam's very much an art lover, Pola. You two should have lots to talk about.

Pola   Do you paint?

Sam   Don't have the time any more. Have to live in the real world, you know. But I like to think I have an artist's eye.

Pola   In a glass jar. No, sorry . . . I'm not taking the piss . . .

Pause.

Sam   Pola, your mother asked us to bring you a little parcel. Unfortunately, Aimee went and left it behind.

Pola   Thank fuck for that. Was it shaped like a small rock by any chance?

Sam   Yes, I think it was as a matter of fact.

Aimee   It'll probably be a crystal like mine.

Pola   An especially big and heavy one. To put round my neck when I go swimming.

Aimee   They're really good, Pola. Very calming. I'll post it on to you as soon as we get back.

Pola   Don't talk about 'getting back', you've only just got here.

Aimee   I'd love to see the caves.

Sam   We could do that tomorrow.

Pola   Yeah, great! . . . oh no . . . not such a good idea . . . unless I can borrow some of your clothes, Aimee.

Aimee   Oh no, you've not got yourself banned?

Pola   I tried to busk in there. The acoustics are great . . . made me sound just like Mariah Carey. Maybe I could dye my hair . . .

Aimee   To look like Mariah Carey?

Pola   So I can get into the caves. I might take my guitar . . .

Aimee   Have you written any more songs?

Pola   Not had the time. Have you written any more poems?

Aimee   No.

Sam   You never told me you're a poet.

Aimee   I'm not.

Pola   Hasn't she written one for you?

Sam   No . . .

Aimee   They're not that good. I'd be embarrassed to show someone who knows anything about poetry.

Pola   They were good enough for me. I'm going to rip them all up now.

Aimee   I just meant they were personal poems . . . sister to sister. They wouldn't be special to anyone else.

Pause.

Pola *moves to take both their cases.* **Sam** *resists.*

Sam   I can manage. It's too heavy for you.

Pola *sweeps the case from* **Sam***, and carries it easily. He tries to give* **Aimee** *a look but she doesn't respond.* **Pola** *takes* **Aimee***'s case too. All three walk off. Sounds of the station recede. Sounds of gulls.*

Pola   See that block? The big grey block of flats there? I live in the smaller block that you can't see behind it. Overlooks the beach – well, the toilet pavilion on the beach. I must show you it . . .

Sam   The toilet pavilion?

Pola   If you're an art lover, Sam, it's unmissable. That exquisite example of early Edwardian shonny boasts some of the best street art in the south-east. Come on, I'll show you.

Sam   I'm not sure 'street art' sounds quite our bag. Give me a gentle watercolour any day . . .

Pola   This is unmissable, Sam, come on . . .

Sam   The sea wind's so biting – and my toes have already gone dead. I think what Aimee and I could most do with, before we go exploring the cultural delights of Hastings, is a cup of coffee and the chance to put our feet up.

Pola   You're tired, Sam?

Sam   Well, just a little.

Pola   I'm sorry. I'm being stupid, I don't think very straight sometimes. A man of your age needs to take things at a more sedate pace.

Sam   I'm not *that* old, Pola.

Pola   It's quite all right. I wouldn't mind putting my feet up too. And it's a very long walk back to my flat.

Aimee   I thought you said in your letter –

Pola   When I said it was near the station I meant the other one.

Sam   Hastings has two stations?

Pola   No, St Leonard's Warrior Square. I thought you'd be getting off there, if you hadn't phoned and said you were coming to Hastings.

Sam   We said Hastings because we thought that was nearer to where you live.

Aimee   We seem to have got our wires crossed.

Sam   Well, we could always pop in somewhere for a quick coffee and a tea cake.

Pola   OK. Cool. Let's walk along the beach.

Sam   Not in these shoes.

Pola   Oh, come on, Sam – get in practice for Cyprus.

She darts ahead.

In here.

She indicates a gap in the dilapidated wooden wall of a building which is in darkness. She disappears through the hole.

Aimee   What's in there?

Pola *reappears.*

Pola   Well, don't hang about out in the cold.

Aimee *and* **Sam** *follow* **Pola** *in.* **Sam** *steps very warily, as if expecting the structure to collapse upon him.*

Pola   This is where I work sometimes. There's seats, a sea view, tea and coffee. Mind your heads.

She switches a light on. **Sam** *and* **Aimee** *look around. They are in an empty amusement arcade.* **Pola** *ushers them to plastic chairs.*

I'll put the kettle on.

Exit **Pola**.

Aimee   What do you think?

Sam   I'm sure I don't know what to think.

Aimee   Do you think I'm like my sister?

Sam   Well, I'm not that sure –

Pola (*off*)   Kettle's on! Biscuits?

Aimee   Yes please!

Enter **Pola** *with a packet of biscuits.*

Pola   They're OK. They've been shut in the tin, so the mice won't have been at them.

Sam *gets up, wanders around the arcade.*

Sam   You say you work *here*?

Pola   Last summer, yeah. In here!

She gets in the little booth for changing money.

Change your money 'ere, mate. You flash it, I'll cash it.

Sam　You really wonder about the kind of people who'd come to a place like this, don't you?

Aimee　It reminds me of our holidays when we were kids.

Pola　Camber Sands.

Aimee　And Eastbourne – do you remember the Butterfly House?

Pola　And Steve . . . and what's-his-name at that disco at Southend?

Aimee　Paul. Paul was mine, Steve was yours and they were playing 'You to Me are Everything' on the dance floor.

Pola　Paul was a rotten kisser.

Aimee　Steve, you mean.

Pola　Do I? Well, maybe. It was years ago.

Aimee　How old were we?

Pola　I was fourteen, so you were just twelve.

Aimee　And we had identical hair.

Pola　And earrings. You wore one of my hoops. I wore one of your little silver crosses.

Aimee *takes her tea and joins* **Sam** *looking around the arcade.*

Aimee　It's a shame this place's closed down for the winter.

Sam　It's so quiet . . . rather eerie . . .

Pola　A surprise, Aimee!

Pola *pulls a lever in the booth. The sound of arcade machines coming to life.*

Aimee　Wow!

She runs to a machine.

Got any change, Sam?

Sam   A waste of money. How much is it anyway?

He looks at the machine and gives her a coin.

Like flushing cash straight down the drain. In my day, they were only a penny a go. You didn't mind that so much. And you at least stood some chance of winning a few bob.

Aimee *is playing the game like a pro.*

Sam   What do you win on these computer things?

Pola   A place on the scoreboard. You'll see my name up there when she gets to the end of the game.

Sam   She has to do what? Zap those little things? It doesn't make much sense. All these games are to do with mindless violence, aren't they? Then the kids grow up and what becomes of them?

Pola   They join Nasa, fully qualified to fly spaceships; some of them become racing drivers, some martial-arts instructors. It's the poor kids who stayed in school you should feel sorry for.

Aimee   Shit, oh shit.

Sam (*disapproving*)   Aimee.

Pola *leans over* **Aimee***'s shoulder.*

Pola   Don't lose your nerve, little Sis. Now! Now! Got 'em.

Sam   How people can become addicted to a cacophony of crude electronic noises and jerky graphics . . .

Aimee   Fuck! Shit! Shot down in flames.

Sam   I suppose these things are indicative of the moronic age we live in.

Aimee   Got any more change, Sam?

Sam 'Got any change?' – you sound like one of those dog-on-a-rope people you insisted on wasting a quid on at East Croydon.

Pola I've been thinking of getting a dog.

Aimee You must, Pola. A great big golden retriever.

Pola All the other buskers have dogs.

Sam You do wonder how they feed them.

Pola In a bowl, I expect.

Aimee *moves to the next game. She takes out her own purse, puts a coin in the machine. Nothing happens.*

Aimee This one's not working.

She presses the buttons on the arcade machine. Suddenly dozens of bars of soap cascade from the money chute.

What . . .

She examines the soap.

Ugh . . . They're all partly used.

Pola You've got to try the grab machine if you want to win something funky.

Sam *looks at the grab machine.* **Pola** *picks up and sniffs a bar of soap.*

Sam You say these prizes are worth the effort? Would you actually wear a pink watch with kittens on the face?

Aimee Melanie next door would love it.

Sam She's had her birthday present. You don't want to be spending all your money on other people's kids.

Pola Look at those jewel-encrusted sunglasses. Unreal. Go for those, Aimee.

Aimee It won't be all my money. Just a couple of goes.

Aimee *goes to put a coin in the machine.*

Pola   Wait. You've not seen everything yet. You've not experienced *all* the atmosphere. You've got to have the full experience before you start playing serious.

Aimee   What's the 'full experience'?

Pola   Shall I sock it to ya?

Pola *presses a button. Loud techno music pounds.* **Sam** *covers his ears.*

Sam   Bloody hell.

Pola   And it goes louder.

She turns the music up.

(Shouting above the din)   And now . . .

She presses another switch. Coloured lights flash on and off.

Sam *(shouts)*   OK, OK! Very nice, I'm sure! Can you switch it off now!

Pola *is dancing energetically.*

Pola   It's terrific, isn't it?

Sam   It's hurting my ears . . . and those lights . . .

Aimee   What, darling?

Aimee *starts dancing too.*

Pola   Cool, isn't it?

Sam   Switch it off now! Please, please.

Pola *and* **Aimee** *dance together.*

Aimee   What?

Sam *makes for the booth. He looks up at the lights, holds his head, clambers into the booth, collapses.* **Pola** *and* **Aimee** *continue dancing for a few moments. Then* **Aimee** *turns, sees* **Sam***. She runs and turns the music off.* **Sam** *is motionless under the eerily pulsating lights.* **Aimee** *and* **Pola** *bend over him.*

Blackout.

Scene Two

Sam and **Aimee** *discovered on, in the arcade.* **Sam** *is motionless, sitting on the floor, slumped forward.* **Pola** *has changed her John Lennon shades to a pair of eye jackets. She reads from a medical encyclopedia.*

Pola   Fits?

Aimee *studies* **Sam**.

Aimee   . . . Maybe.

Pola   Epileptic?

Aimee   He'd have told me.

Pola   Catatonic?

Aimee   What's that?

Pola (*reading*)   'The patient may seem totally out of touch with his surroundings.'

She walks around **Sam** *reading from the book.*

Pola   'He may pass into a kind of trance where he is still as a statue.'

Aimee   And?

Pola   That's all. It's a shit book.

Aimee   Doesn't it say what to do?

Pola   'Ring Mother for advice.' No, it doesn't say anything else. Hang on, what's this? – There's catalepsy too – 'a hysterical or self-induced trance'.

Aimee   Sam isn't the hysterical type.

Pola   What *is* he like?

Aimee   He's very nice . . .

Pola   He's not as bad as I'd feared. What's he like in bed?

Aimee   If you think I'm discussing –

Pola   Too bad. Still you can't have everything.

She laughs.

It's freaky, us talking as if he's not there. Fuck, fuck, fuck. (*In* **Sam***'s ear.*) Fuck. It feels really weird saying 'fuck' in front of guys like Sam.

Aimee   What do you mean? Sam hears me swearing all the time.

Pola   Doesn't it feel a bit like . . . saying 'balls' to the vicar?

Aimee   Sam swears too.

Pola   Not any more.

Aimee   You're horrible!

Pola   Hate you.

She offers **Aimee** *the biscuits.*

Sure you won't have another biscuit?

Aimee   We've got to call someone. Maybe I should ring Mum after all.

Pola   The ambulance's on its way. Time she gets on the next train down from Sydenham, he'll be safely at the hospital.

Aimee   Nothing like this has ever happened to him before . . .

Pola *studies* **Sam** *from beneath her beret.*

Pola   As far as you know. Cup of tea?

She takes the front off one of the arcade machines. Lots of empty wine and spirit bottles roll out on to the floor. She reaches further inside and pulls out a couple of mugs and a box of tea bags.

There's no sugar, I'm afraid.

Aimee   I don't take sugar now.

Pola   Because of him?

Aimee   Because of my weight. Look at me.

Pola   I am. You're still a string bean, Aimee.

Enter **Jake**. *He is unaware of the girls. He starts rubbing the hull of the boat with sandpaper.*

Pola *stands in front of* **Sam**. **Aimee** *goes and looks out at* **Jake**. **Pola** *flashes her tits at* **Sam**. *No reaction.* **Pola** *stands behind* **Aimee**. *As* **Aimee** *turns,* **Pola** *puts her finger to her lips.*

Aimee   He might know what to do. He might be a lifeguard or something.

Pola   Right . . . Does he look like a lifeguard?

Aimee   Well . . .

Pola   He looks like a scumbag.

Aimee (*hushed*)   Do you know him?

Jake *looks around him; he's forgotten something. He stands up and exits.*

Pola   Shhh. Stay here.

She creeps outside. She takes a felt-tip pen from her pocket, draws a big 'W' on the side of the boat. She rushes back inside as **Jake** *enters with a can of paint, and a jar containing brushes.*

How's Sydenham?

Aimee   I don't think the station staff miss you.

Pola   I kept them in work. They should've been queuing to shake my hand. Is much of my writing left on the wall?

Aimee   It's all been painted out on both platforms. But your multicoloured trackside tag at Penge West is still looking good.

Jake *tries unsuccessfully to lift the lid on the paint can. He exits again as* **Pola** *darts out, draws a fat 'A' on the boat. She darts back in.* **Jake** *returns with a knife to prise open the paint can.*

Aimee   What address did you give them?

Pola   Who?

Aimee   Emergency services.

Pola   This one.

Aimee   It's been nearly an hour!

Pola   Don't clock-watch.

Aimee   Act like I don't care?

Pola   Stop caring.

Aimee   I wish I was like you.

Pola   High as a kite?

Aimee   Practical.

Pola   That's what older sisters are for.

Aimee   I wish we'd gone straight back to the flat.

Pola   Flat? I thought you'd twigged.

Pause.

I live here. The shit about the flat was all for him. (*Indicates* **Sam**.) Had to show him I'm good for something. I did have that flat, the one I pointed out, but can't pay, won't pay, out you go, baby. I still go back and collect my post from my pigeon-hole. And I brought the phone with me. Now it's on somebody else's bill. Cool.

Aimee   Don't you get benefits?

Pola   Of what? Yeah, amphetamines are very competitively priced down here. If I do get a dog what shall I call him? I had thought of naming him Sam, but that doesn't seem so funny now. 'Here, Sam. Here, boy'. A bit sick, isn't it?

Jake *starts sanding the boat again. Pause.*

Pola   He's giving it a good old rub, isn't he?

Aimee   Pola, Mum said . . .

Pola   Mum said! I know everything Mum can possibly have said by heart.

Aimee   She worries.

Pola   She'll give herself an irritable bowel. Irritable bowel – you know what that means, Aimee? Every time you shit, your arsehole tells you to fuck off.

Aimee   It's so good to see you.

She takes off **Pola***'s sunglasses.*

You must come and visit us in Cyprus.

Pola   How can I afford that?

Aimee   I'm sure Sam would –

Pola *puts her hand over* **Aimee***'s mouth.*

Pola   Don't say it. I don't want his money. He doesn't like me.

Aimee   He does.

Pola   Did he say so?

Aimee   He didn't have a chance. But I'm sure he would've if I'd asked him.

Pola   Yeah, I'm sure he can lie as well as anyone.

Aimee   Why do you always think people hate you?

Pola *leaves* **Aimee***, goes to fiddle with one of the arcade machines.* **Aimee** *rests her arm on* **Sam***'s shoulder. He slumps sideways. She jumps.*

Aimee   Oh, what are we going to do? I wish I'd studied first aid.

Pola   We did resuscitating dummies at school – same difference.

Aimee   But Sam's still breathing.

Pola   Well, we know what to do if he stops.

Aimee   At least he hasn't swallowed his tongue.

Pola   Can you really do that . . . to yourself?

She pulls a face trying.

You're kidding me. (*Indicating* **Jake**.) Now if we're talking long tongues, that guy could make the record books.

Aimee   Him? You *do* know him?

Pola   Sure. I've seen him eating an ice cream.

She collects up some bars of soap.

His name's Jake. And one of these is his.

Aimee   Is that his boat?

Jake *is now putting some elbow grease into rubbing the hull of the boat.*

Pola   He thinks it's his dick. Look at him. Faster, faster, yes, oh yes . . . (*Looks at* **Aimee**.) . . . oh, oh, ow, oooh baby.

Aimee   I'd love to have a boat.

Pola   I thought you were going to say you'd love to have a dick.

Aimee *goes over to* **Sam**.

Aimee   Maybe we should check they're really sending an ambulance.

Pola   Of course they are, baby. Right now, somewhere in the midst of Hastings General some frail little octogenarian's being turfed out of her bed to make way for your precious Sammy.

Aimee   Maybe you should've mentioned he's with BUPA.

Sound of a siren. **Pola** *picks up her guitar.*

Here it comes!

Pola (*sings over the sound of the siren*)   Here it comes. Here it comes. Here comes your nineteenth nervous breakdown.

Sound of an ambulance speeding past. **Aimee** *cries out in frustration.*

Aimee   No!

Pola   Maybe it was a request stop.

She puts down the guitar, goes and puts her arms around **Aimee**.

Oh, baby. The next one will be ours, you'll see.

Aimee   Suppose they got the address wrong? You did give it to them correctly. You didn't get confused?

Pola   Me? Hey, who was the Girl Guide here, hey?

Aimee   For two weeks. This is a nightmare, a complete fucking nightmare.

Aimee *is in tears.* **Pola** *hugs her.*

Pola   Hey, now. The ambulance won't be long, trust me. Probably like the buses in Sydenham, nothing for an hour, then three turn up at once. Oh, hush now, hey.

Aimee   I should take off my crystal.

Pola   What? Yes, I should. It must be exhausting carting that great lump of rock around. Now me, I like my jewellery subtle.

Aimee   You don't know the meaning of subtle.

Pola   Small and boring.

Aimee   Anyway, it's not jewellery, it's functional . . . therapeutic. I really think there's something in this crystal healing thing.

She tears her pendant off.

I dropped it yesterday. Chipped it. I think that's what's been affecting my energy levels.

Pola   If Mother told you there were fairies at the bottom of our garden, would you buy it, Aimee?

Aimee   Why do you always want to take the piss out of Mum? /You know she cares –

Pola   /Because I hate her!

Aimee   No! (*Pause.*) Oh why do you have to be like this!

Aimee *sobs again.* **Pola** *goes to her.*

Pola   Oh hey. Aimee. It's a personal thing, that's all. Some people get on, some don't. It's just a little personal thing . . .

She holds **Aimee**, *sits her down on her knee, rocking her.*

Hush now . . . hey . . .

Pause. She picks up her guitar again.

Corn-baked yellow in the hot sun. Remember? I've written you a tune for it.

She strums the guitar and sings.

> Corn-baked yellow in the hot sun
> Sunshine poem, sunshine song
> The honeysuckle slowly opens
> Rock roses and buttercups.

> Furry bees are drinking nectar
> Sunshine poem, sunshine song
> In the café gleaming bottles
> Cast soft rainbows on the wall.

Pola *plays the guitar, quietly, intimately, looking into* **Aimee**'s *face. When she begins to sing again,* **Aimee** *joins in, knowing the words of her poem, though the tune is new to her.*

> The orange juice drips pinky-peach
> Sunshine poem, sunshine song
> Fills my glass with dappled sunspots
> Swirling gold and copper prisms.

The sun dips down towards the waves
Aimee's poem, Pola's song
Sunshine melting in ruby drops
Turns the sea florid crimson.

Aimee*'s attention switches back to* **Sam**. *She gets up off* **Pola***'s lap, breaking the spell.* **Pola** *jumps up.*

Pola   Smelling salts. It might just be a faint. If it is, we're going to look a couple of right Mandys rushing him into intensive care.

Aimee   Have you got any?

Pola   Smelling salts? Only thing I've ever sniffed is deodorant.

Aimee   Why did we used to do that?

Pola   We were worried about our nostrils sweating? Shit, we must've been like part of this big Sydenham Rightguard-sniffing thing in the eighties. Nostalgia, it does your head in. Where would I get these smelling salts?

Aimee   Boots?

Pola   Yeah . . . Boots *cares*. Cool. In the precinct. I'll drop some of my bottles in the sea on the way . . .

She picks up a few bottles, puts them in a carrier bag.

I collect them at high tide, dry them out, and put a message in each of them. It's kinda like long-distance tagging.

Aimee   I thought when I saw all these you must have a drink problem. Do you get many replies?

Pola   Yeah . . . from kids and idiots. I send the kids a few sweets cos they all think they're in for some kind of prize for finding the bottle. I usually ignore the idiots. I'll just get my other shades.

Aimee   The sun's not even shining.

Pola   You can't see ultraviolet rays, Aimee.

She fetches three pairs of sunglasses, and tries them all.

The foxy-lady look. Or my eye jackets – funky! . . . Do you
think? These are quite retro. Yes? No?

Aimee (*distractedly*)   Nice yeah.

Pola *puts two pairs of sunglasses in her pocket, one pair on her face.
She picks up the bottles again, kisses* **Aimee***'s cheek.*

Pola   See ya.

Exit **Pola***.*

Blackout.

Scene Three

Sam *is lying on the floor at the front of the arcade.* **Aimee** *switches
the arcade music on. Now it's that Lisa Loeb song, 'I Miss You'.*
Aimee *drags her suitcase around behind an arcade machine to change
her outfit. While she changes,* **Aimee** *sings along, 'You say, I only
hear what I want to,' hums a bit, 'cos I miss you, yeah, yeah I miss
you.'*

Jake *stops work, looks up, listens. He smiles, goes to the entrance of
the arcade.*

Jake (*calls out*)   Someone having a party in there?

Aimee (*calls back*)   No.

Jake   So what ya doing?

Aimee   One minute. Wait there, OK?

Aimee *finishes changing.*

Jake (*still outside*)   Sure.

He peers through the boards, but does not see **Sam***, lying in the
shadow, or* **Aimee***.* **Aimee** *emerges from behind the arcade machine
wearing a floaty shift dress and high heels. She switches the music off,*

ducks through the doorway, blinking in the bright light as she emerges. **Jake** *leans nonchalantly against the wall of the arcade.*

Hello. Have we met?

Aimee   No.

Aimee *looks past him.*

Jake   Are you waiting for the man, or might someone else do?

Aimee   I'm waiting for my sister. Is it far to Boots?

Jake   Not very. If you cross the road, take the first left –

Aimee   I have to wait here. For the ambulance.

Jake   Right . . .

Aimee   She's been gone ages . . .

Jake   . . . An ambulance, you said? Are you all right, I mean –

Aimee   Oh come and look at him!

Jake *follows* **Aimee** *into the arcade. He sees* **Sam***, quickly goes to him, motions to* **Aimee** *to keep back, but is unwilling to touch* **Sam** *himself.*

Jake   Shit!

He looks at **Aimee***, expecting an explanation. She remains staring at* **Sam***.*

You just found him lying here, right?

Aimee   He's my fiancé.

Jake   Oh. (*Pause.*) Is he –

Aimee   He's had a bad turn.

Jake *nervously touches* **Sam***, then checks his pulse, and other signs of life.*

Jake   He's completely out of it. What happened?

Aimee   Pola was showing us how the lights and music work.

Jake   Pola?

Aimee   My sister.

Jake   Was it a strobe?

Aimee   Eh? No . . .

Jake   Laser?

Aimee   Just coloured bulbs, I think.

Jake *switches the lights on.*

Aimee   Don't.

Jake *(sarkily)*   Unbearable, isn't it?

Aimee   If it was the lights, they might make him worse.

Jake *turns the lights off.*

Aimee   We put him in the recovery position, but he hasn't.

Jake   He might've taken something. Unless maybe he's on some kind of medication already and that's what –

Aimee   He's really proud about how he's not been to a doctor in ten years . . .

Jake   He's had one too many maybe . . .

Aimee   He's teetotal!

Jake   Yeah? Yeah, he looks the type. Did he touch any electric wires? – electric shock.

Aimee   No.

Jake   Has anything happened to him today? – ordinary shock.

Aimee   No . . . er, he thinks we were ripped off over the sandwiches on the train but that wouldn't . . . no, sorry, I'm rambling.

Jake   Look, why don't you come and sit down . . .

He leads **Aimee** *to a seat.*

It's no good getting yourself in a state now, is it? Take some deep breaths of the nice salty air. That's it.

Pause.

Allergies.

Aimee   What?

Jake   Has he got any allergies? Like . . . peanuts? milk? . . . sandwiches?

Aimee   No.

Jake   Must've been the lights then. Maybe he's just a really sensitive guy.

Aimee   Yes. He says he's sensitive.

Jake   Don't we all? And the girls still buy it.

He fiddles with the arcade machine.

Have you had a go on this?

Aimee   Yeah.

Jake   Did you see my name among the high scores?

Pause. **Aimee** *looks at* **Sam**.

So, you're Pola's sister, you said.

Aimee *looks at* **Jake** *with more interest.*

Aimee   You know her?

Jake   Everyone knows Pola.

Aimee   She's lots of friends down here?

Enter **Pola** *without* **Jake** *or* **Aimee** *noticing. She is carrying a bag. She crouches behind* **Jake**'*s boat and completes writing 'WANKER' on it. She starts to colour the letters in.*

Jake   She's really popular.

Aimee   That's good.

Jake   Yeah, everyone has a tale to tell.

Aimee   About my sister? What are they saying?

Jake   . . . Ah . . . that she's fun to be with, a good laugh . . . She used to be part of this gang . . . last summer, spraying grafitti on stations.

Aimee   She's been doing that for years.

Jake   And train surfing – hanging on to a train door as it gathers speed and moves out of the platform. One night I was on the last train back from Brighton and she was suspended in some kind of home-made harness, dangling over the footbridge adding to some multicoloured piece of art on the brickwork. Another time I saw her painting on the roof of a train in a siding.

Aimee   I wish she'd hurry. How long does it take to buy one item?

Jake   She's probably bumped into someone she knows . . .

Aimee   She knows it's an emergency.

Jake   Good point.

Aimee *stands over* **Sam**.

Aimee   Oh, I can't bear this. Look at him! I never imagined a man like him would ever look at me . . . And now he won't. I'm like all those songs and programmes he switches off because they're 'not to his taste'.

Jake   You been together a long time then?

Aimee   Nearly a year. He's my boss. I had to leave my old job cos of harassment . . . I've always felt safe with Sam.

He's more like a big . . . (*stops herself*) . . . he's a really nice bloke.

Jake   Yeah. (*Pause.*) Yeah, he looks it. What's he do?

Aimee   Works for a travel firm. We're about to move to Cyprus . . . and get married.

Jake   Nice.

Aimee   That's if . . . well if he's OK . . . we were leaving next week.

Jake   So nothing like this has ever happened to him before?

Aimee   No, and we've been through the medical book from A to Z. I thought I knew everything about him. I mean, we discuss everything – bills, holidays, whether to go to friends' parties – we never do . . . not if they're my friends, at any rate. The trouble I had persuading him to come down here for the weekend . . .

Jake   He doesn't like your friends?

Aimee   Because they're not like him, I suppose. I mean, he's been to university . . . no it's not that. He's more used to mixing with . . . I don't know . . . people like him.

Jake   So, you don't have much in common.

Aimee   Sometimes I look at him and I know he's upset or angry with me. He doesn't say anything but I can see it in his face, and I don't know what I've done.

Jake   Why don't you ask him?

Aimee   He says 'it's nothing', but I can see in his eyes that he has contempt for me . . . no, I'm sorry, that's not what I mean. That was a shitty thing to say . . . when he's just lying there.

The pause gets uncomfortable.

Jake   I'm sorry I haven't even asked –

Aimee   Aimee. You're Jake, I know. Pola's mentioned you.

Jake   Yeah? I meant to call her.

Aimee   So did I.

The sound of a siren, faint. She goes to the door, spots **Pola**.

Aimee   Hey! What're you doing? – where's the smelling salts?

Pola *gets up, comes in with the bag of 'shopping'. She sees* **Jake**, *thrusts the bag into* **Aimee**'s *arms.*

Pola (*to* **Jake**)   Get out of here.

Jake   I've missed you.

Pola   Get the fuck out!

Jake *moves to go.* **Pola** *blocks his way.*

Pola   And take your soap with you.

Jake   Soap?

Pola *indicates the pile of soap.*

Pola   It's there somewhere.

Jake   Wait, I don't . . . You stole my soap?

Aimee *takes from the bag a furry hot-water bottle case, a packet of sore-mouth pastilles, a pair of socks and an empty CD box.*

Pola   Yours and the other bastards who didn't call me.

Pause. **Jake** *stares at the soap.*

Jake   All of these . . .

Pola   . . . Said they'd call.

Aimee *rummages in the bottom of the bag.*

Aimee   Pola . . . why did you buy all this stuff?

Pola   I didn't.

Aimee *finds the smelling salts in the bottom of the bag. She unscrews the lid, sniffs them.*

Aimee   Shit! It's really foul . . . it'll probably make him worse.

Pola   Just stick it under his nose.

Aimee *puts the smelling salts under* **Sam**'s *nose.*

Aimee   Oh . . . oh no!

Jake *and* **Pola** *join her.*

Pola   What he do?

Aimee   Nothing. No reaction. He feels cold.

Jake   Shit.

Pola *and* **Jake** *check* **Sam**'s *signs of life.*

Pola   His breathing's fine. He does feel a bit chilly, but he's not shivering.

Aimee   Perhaps he can't. Can you shiver when you're unconscious?

Pola   Fuck knows. Have you found your soap? It's one thing to forget to call someone when you said you would, but quite another to forget what your own soap looks like. What colour was it?

Jake *crouches, looking at the soap.*

Jake   Sometimes I have Lifebuoy . . .

Aimee   That's red or white usually.

Jake   Or Palmolive.

Aimee   Pale green.

Jake   But it might've been a coal tar one.

Aimee   Golden yellow.

Pola   He doesn't have a clue.

Aimee (*to* **Pola**)   Can you remember?

Pola   Oh you bet. I reckon I could identify each of them blindfold, by texture, shape and smell . . . which is more than I could their owners. I'm thinking of melting them all down and making one huge multicoloured bar. When I eventually get a place with my own bath, I can lie back in the tub and imagine all the sights it's seen . . . and the places it's been.

Jake   So that's it . . .

Aimee   You've found it?

Jake   Every time I've walked in the pub, one of the lads has made a joke about whether I've washed lately. So everyone knows about it? . . . Or are they all in the same position?

Pola   It's not your problem. *You said you'd call.*

Jake   *I've been busy.*

Pola   Bollocks.

Jake   I'm sorry. I've dropped by once or twice.

Pola   While I was out? How convenient. Heard it before.

Jake   I'm sorry, Pola. Look . . . why don't we go for a drink –

Pola   Believe it or not, it's not a good time.

Jake   I mean later . . .

Pola   Yeah, later. You'll call me. Fine.

Jake *goes back to his boat, sees the writing on it.*

Jake   Oy! Hey, you . . .

Pola *strolls over to the boat.*

Pola   Mindless vandalism. Is nothing sacred?

Jake   You think I can't recognise your handiwork?

Pola   Are you making allegations? Mind you, it must be someone who knows you, to be able to provide such an accurate character assessment . . .

Sam *moves slightly.* **Aimee** *gasps.*

Aimee   He moved! Pola!

Pola *and* **Jake** *rush to join* **Aimee** *who is looking at* **Sam**.

Aimee   Sam. Sam!

Blackout.

Scene Four

Pola *is sitting beside* **Sam**, *who is lying on his back. She has put her sunglasses and beret on him. Beside them is a large, empty glass jar and a little pile of shells. Outside,* **Jake** *is painting the boat.* **Aimee** *sits beside him.*

Pola (*to* **Sam**)   I'd love to get away from all the insincere shit happening around me. I'd love to travel like Aimee says you have.

She pushes a shell into his hand, holds it up to 'show' him.

This shell's from Madagascar! In the deep blue Indian ocean. It must have washed up on the silvery sand of a tropical beach. A hermit crab used it for his home. A ring-tailed lemur darted down from a tree, scooped him out with a paw and ate him for her dinner. Oh, I expect you've opened an hotel there and can tell me I'm talking bollocks – there were no crabs or lemurs and the shell's probably made of plastic.

She begins to put the shells back in the jar.

Still, I say one thing for you, Sam. You're a good listener. And that's rare in a man. But you're still like most of your sort, even though travel is supposed to broaden your mind.

Pola *lifts* **Sam**'s *head to address him. She takes his hand to his face, runs one of his fingers around his lips, then bends to suck his finger.*

The look on your face when we met earlier . . . you're certainly not broad-minded, are you? When you're travelling you must see plenty of beggars and plenty of whores. And that's the look you give them too, isn't it? That genteel look of civilised disgust. Then you make them grovel for a coin in the dust or turn tricks for a lousy couple of quid.

Pola *gets up and leaves* **Sam**.

Aimee   So you've been all over?

Jake   All over the Med, yeah. Working on other people's boats. Fixing the engines, giving them an overhaul. Anywhere there's an ocean, boats and people willing to pay cash, that's where I'll be.

Aimee   I've never been abroad.

Jake   No shit.

Aimee   Moving to Cyprus with Sam was going to be my first time out of the country.

Jake   He'll get better. You'll still be able to go.

Aimee *looks back at* **Pola**.

Aimee   I'd been getting quite anxious about it. Stupid, I know. Sam says homesickness is a myth as long as it's dreary old Britain you're leaving behind.

Pola *strolls out to them.*

Aimee   The colour and life of the Mediterranean, the beaches, the views, the history of the place will soon have us wondering how we could've ever lived anywhere else . . .

Pola   /I miss Sydenham/

Aimee   . . . Sitting outside a little café on the quay, listening to the chatter of the locals –

Pola   But not understanding much of it.

Aimee   In a couple of months, Sam says, we'll *be* locals in Famagusta. Sitting under a sun-umbrella, plates piled high with a banquet of lobster, prawn and . . . do you think they'll have vegetarian places?

Pause.

I . . . do you think we should give the hospital another ring?

Pola   Sure, I'll go and call them.

Aimee   I don't mind. Phone's in the room at the back, you said?

Pola   I'll go. I can be more firm and forceful about it.

Aimee   Perhaps you overdid it a bit and they didn't believe you.

Pola   You can't just say 'Please send me an ambulance, if you've got the time, and it's really no trouble'.

Jake   Yeah, don't forget to tell them you'll be consulting a solicitor. You've got to let them know you could get seriously legal on their arses.

Pola   Won't be long.

Pola *goes back in the arcade.* **Jake** *hands* **Aimee** *a paint brush. Backs to the arcade, they start to paint the boat.* **Pola** *fetches her phone.*

Aimee   I don't know what I'd do without her. I'm always hopeless in emergencies.

Jake   She's how much older, if you don't mind me asking?

Aimee   Three years. We both still lived at home until last year. Pola and Mum were always rowing. Finally Pola just left – packed and went without saying goodbye. We were so worried. So were the hospital. Months went by and nothing. Then one day I got a call . . . from Hastings.

Jake I'm a Hastings man born and bred. My dad was a boat builder, so was his dad.

Aimee If I had a little boat like this I'd go sailing round the coast.

Jake All by yourself?

Aimee *looks towards the arcade and* **Pola** *again.*

Aimee Mmmm. Maybe.

Pola *turns her attention to* **Sam** *again.*

Pola You know Mother will really love this, Sam. She was so delighted Aimee had found someone normal, someone sane. Someone not like Dad and me. And now look at you! You're the nutter, Sammy.

Aimee I'd better tell her to mention BUPA this time.

Pola *climbs astride* **Sam***, sliding down his body.*

Pola And when we first met I'd never have guessed. I thought successful guys like you were invincible, untouchable. I didn't used to think of suits like you as human at all. Mind you, now you're not really human any more, are you? You're more of a vegetable . . . like a lettuce, Sam, or a big cucumber, eh?

She gets off **Sam***. She toys with the telephone.*

I don't know if I can risk calling an ambulance for someone like you. What have your sort ever done for anyone like me? One less person like you, a little more wealth will be shared among us. One gram of privilege will be broken up and sprinkled down upon people like me.

She dials. **Aimee** *comes in behind her without* **Pola** *noticing.*

(*On phone.*) It's Pola. Cheese and tomato, twelve-inch, deep-pan. Right. Terrific.

She puts the phone down, turns to see **Aimee** *standing in the doorway.*

Pola   Ambulance is on its way.

Aimee   What did they say?

Pola   Oh, the usual. And apologised for the delay

Aimee *sits down beside* **Sam**. **Jake** *comes in, joins* **Pola**.

Jake   I hope you gave the hospital a real bollocking. It's disgusting. You'll definitely have grounds to sue. So how long did they say they're going to be, this time?

Aimee *looks at* **Pola**.

Pola   I told them it's a *really* urgent emergency. So they said they could try to make it in twenty minutes . . . as his condition is so serious . . . and he's with BUPA.

Aimee   It's too long.

Pola   Shall I phone them back and try to haggle a bit? 'Ten minutes. Fifteen's our last offer. Twelve, take it or leave it. Thirteen, just for you.'

Aimee   It would be quicker to get a cab.

Pola   You have to phone for one down here. They don't come for ages, and they're really expensive. Have you got enough money for a taxi, Aimee? Me, I'm skint.

Jake   My wallet's in my other trousers.

Aimee   How far's the hospital anyway?

Jake   About a ten-minute walk.

Pola   Oh yeah, there's a sign pointing there further along the road. I've carefully painted around the word 'hospital' so people can still read it in emergencies.

Jake   Very public-spirited.

Aimee   So couldn't we just carry him there?

Jake   Well, yeah . . . I reckon we could manage him between us, no hassle. Or flag down a car if he gets too heavy.

Pola   Nice idea, but look, we've got an ambulance on its way.

Aimee   In twenty minutes' time. Supposing this one doesn't stop either? Supposing they're twenty-five minutes, or half an hour . . . he could be on the ward receiving treatment if we took him there ourselves.

Jake   OK, let's carry him.

Pola   Wait a minute . . .

Aimee   Yes, just let me put my flat shoes on.

Aimee *goes to the back of the arcade, changes her shoes.*

Pola   What's she gone and got herself all dressed up for anyway?

Jake   Perhaps she thinks we're going to get filmed for *Blues and Twos* or some other ambulance-chasing programme. It's a shame Sam's not a dog or a cat. We might get to meet Rolf Harris.

Pola   Not in Hastings.

Jake *and* **Pola** *wait, looking at* **Sam**.

Pola   He doesn't like me.

Jake   How on earth can you tell? By the way his lip's curling?

Pola   It was curling when he arrived. The moment he first set eyes on me.

Jake   You can't expect everyone to fall at your feet.

Pola   I didn't say he doesn't fancy me.

Jake   Shag your sister's bloke . . . would you?

Pola   How could you even think such a thing? I prefer my men to be slightly more lively.

Pause.

What do you think of her?

Jake Aimee? I told you, she's nice.

Pola Lots of people are nice.

Jake Not in the way she is. He's a lucky bloke . . . well, before this whole thing happened, I mean.

Pause.

Look, if they do reconstruct this for that *999* programme – do you get paid, I wonder?

Aimee *rejoins them in flat shoes.*

Aimee Have you a blanket or anything? It's getting really cold.

Pola I've got a big old coat I bought from a charity shop and never wear cos it smells funny . . .

Aimee It'll do.

Pola *fetches the coat, holds it up for* **Jake** *and* **Aimee** *to sniff. It does smell pretty bad.*

Jake Fuckin' hell! He'll be knocking 'em dead at casualty.

Jake *and* **Aimee** *wrap the coat around* **Sam**.

Pola I've put the kettle on for another cuppa.

Aimee I don't think we should hang about.

She picks up the furry hot-water bottle.

But you could fill the hottie. That'll keep him warm.

Exit **Pola** *with the hot-water bottle.*

Aimee It's good of you to help us.

Jake No problem.

Aimee You really like her?

Jake She's a nice girl.

Aimee   She never meets anyone . . . you know . . . nice.
Anyone who'd be good for her.

Jake   Like Sam's good for you?

*Enter **Pola** with the filled hot-water bottle. She tucks it inside the coat
wrapped around **Sam**.*

Pola   There. Snug as a bug in a rug.

Aimee   We're going to take you up the hospital now,
Sam. Don't worry, they'll soon put you to rights.

Jake   Ready then? I'll take the head end, you girls grab his
feet.

Jake *lifts **Sam** into a sitting position.*

Pola   Wait! Wait, watch what you're doing. You're
bending his back! I really think you'd better wait for the
experts. You'll make things worse. He'll end up paralysed or
something.

Aimee   We'll be careful. We've already moved him a few
times. (*To **Jake**.*) We tried lying him on one side, sitting him
up, lying him down again . . .

Pola   And did it help? Did it hell.

Jake   It's not as if he's got broken bones.

Pola   Oh, so you're the expert suddenly. You weren't here
when he fell. He hit the deck quite hard. He could have
injured his back, or his neck.

Jake   Well, we'll be really careful then, won't we? A leg
each girls. Now lift him up. Nice and easy.

*They lift **Sam**.*

Aimee   Slowly, carefully.

Pola   Oh God, his leg feels funny!

Pola *puts **Sam**'s leg down.*

Jake   Well, swap it for the one Aimee's got.

Aimee *and* **Pola** *swap legs.*

Aimee   He'll be all right, Pola. Don't worry.

They carry **Sam** *to the front of the arcade.* **Pola** *and* **Aimee** *head in opposite directions, making* **Sam** *do the splits.*

Jake   Let's decide on a common direction, people.

Pola   It's this way.

Jake   Here we go.

Exit **Pola**, **Aimee** *and* **Jake** *with* **Sam**.

Blackout.

Scene Five

Enter **Jake**, **Pola** *and* **Aimee** *carrying* **Sam**.

Aimee   It's lucky we passed that sign or we might still be going the wrong way.

Jake   I told you, Pola. What did I tell you?

Pola   I got confused. I started thinking of somewhere else. I don't like to think of hospitals for any length of time.

Aimee   Well, we're nearly there now, aren't we?

Jake   Thank fuck, he's quite a weight, your Sammy. And you know what's beginning to worry me? I mean, no offence but how sure can we be that he's still in full control of all his bodily functions?

Aimee   You've got nothing to worry about. You've got his head end. Anyway, it's not very nice to talk about my Sam like that. None of this is his fault . . .

Pola   Look, I . . . I'm going to have to leave you here.

Jake   What!

Pola   I'd promised I'd go and see someone.

Aimee Who?

Pola Just someone. I told you I was busy this weekend.
I told you it wasn't really convenient to have guests . . .
I promised I'd go and look at a litter of puppies this
evening . . .

Aimee Can't you go later?

Pola All the best ones will be gone. I'll probably end up
with some really mangy, flea-bitten dog and it'll be your
fault. Anyway, there's nothing I can do at the hospital. I
hate hospitals. They'll probably be straight on the phone to
my hospital. And my hospital will tell them to keep me
there –

Aimee (*interrupts*) No they won't, Pola.

Jake Are you just going to leave me holding him like this
all night?

Pola You know what that hospital did to me, Aimee. You
know what they did to Dad.

Aimee They tried to help him.

Pola Then why is he dead, Aimee? I know you were too
young to understand. And you believed every line that
Mother fed to you. First, she put him in there, and they
killed him. Then she put me in there.

Aimee Pola!

Pola I'll . . . I'll get a really nice puppy, Aimee. When you
get back, we can take him down on the beach and train
him.

Aimee Pola, you can't just –

Pola I've got to go now. See you.

Exit **Pola**, *running.*

Aimee Pola!

Jake   Crazy cow. We can manage him between the two of us. Come on, Aimee, it's not far now. One, two, three, up he comes.

Exit **Jake** *and* **Aimee** *with* **Sam**.

Blackout.

Act Two

Scene One

*Lights up on **Aimee** and **Jake** sitting on chairs with **Sam** between them. Fade up hospital-type sounds — feet walking down a corridor, etc.*

Aimee   They just think he's had one too many!

Jake   Drunken trash – Back of the queue.

Aimee   If Sam was able to speak for himself this wouldn't have happened. He'd have half a dozen specialists fussing over him. I forgot to mention BUPA again. Next time a nurse walks by, I'll tell her.

Jake   Last time I was up here was last New Year's Eve. I'd been out with a few mates. On our way to the fourth pub in our little pilgrimage I thought it might be a bit of a laugh to vault a concrete bollard . . .

Aimee   Oh no . . . don't tell me . . .

Jake   That's right – clobbered myself right in the goolies, didn't I? My mates managed to carry me up to casualty and we sat there for four hours. You'd never seen anything like it. It was like a bloody battlefield. The prime of Hastings' young manhood lying all over the ground, all felled in a single night's action. Some were still fighting where they'd fallen, on a floor slippery with lager –

Aimee   I think I get the picture.

Jake   There was this poor guy standing in the middle of all this carnage – wild-eyed, staring at the ceiling just saying, 'Oh fuck, oh fuck', over and over again. A nurse goes up to him and she calls him 'doctor' and drags him off to see to some poor sod who'd thrown up over his own feet. I told the guys to carry me home.

Aimee   So you didn't even get seen by a doctor?

Jake That's the funny thing – on the way home, we passed Steers, a nightclub under the cliffs. The music was pounding, and a whole group of girl students were just going in the door, with skirts up here . . . Well . . . we went in, I got chatting to one of the girls, turns out she's a medical student, home for the hols, so eventually I did get seen to . . . so to speak. God, we could be sat here for hours.

Aimee You've been very kind, but you needn't stop. We'll be OK now.

Jake I'll just wait until you've got someone taking care of him.

Aimee Thanks, Jake. Do you think I could ask another favour?

Jake Now that might be stretching it . . .

Aimee Would you keep an eye on Pola for me?

Jake I don't know where she's gone.

Aimee I mean, when I've gone . . . to Cyprus . . . or back to Sydenham.

Jake Sure.

Aimee Sometimes Pola starts feeling a bit down . . .

Jake Don't we all?

Aimee Certain thoughts get into her head . . . about people hating her, about life not being worth living . . .

Jake My doctor gave me Prozac. My dad died – drowned while fishing. Then Joanne dumped me. The cat decided to live with someone else . . .

Aimee I'm sorry.

Jake My flat got burgled. A guy broke my nose. A DSS person saw me working . . .

Aimee I'm really sorry . . .

Jake   That's just life, isn't it?

Pause.

Aimee   I'd kill for a KitKat or a Crunchie.

Jake   They ought to bring round a sweet trolley. A mini McDonald's on wheels would be cool.

Aimee   You'd think some enterprising individual would've thought of it.

Jake   I could nip down the corridor, see if there's a drinks machine or anything.

Aimee   You're a hero.

Jake   No trouble, lady.

Jake *gets up.*

Aimee   You know, I can understand why Pola hates hospitals. It's really depressing just sitting here. They ought to get local artists to paint the walls or something.

Exit **Jake**.

The hiss of a spray can in the dark. **Aimee** *leans against* **Sam**. *Lights down on all but* **Aimee** *and* **Sam**. *Hospital noises fade.*

Enter **Jake**. *In the darkness,* **Jake** *looks around.*

Jake   Pola? Is that you?

Pola, *crouching in shadows by the wall, presses the trigger on an empty aerosol. The hiss of a little escaping propellant.*

Jake   So you decided not to desert us after all.

Another hiss of paint.

Jake   The air reeks of spray-paint. Hope it's CFC-free, or you'll have made a hole in the ozone layer big enough for the Martians to watch Hastings FC when they're playing at home. Pola?

He stalks **Pola**. *She backs away.*

Where are you .-. . ?

Pola *knocks against something.*

Jake   I can see you.

Jake *stalks* **Pola***, then veers off away from her. Stealthily, he creeps up on* **Pola** *from behind, grabs hold of her. She shrieks.*

Pola   You're a monster!

Jake   Where's this puppy then?

Pola *struggles free.*

Pola   Woof! The man wanted too much money for them.

Jake   I'm taking orders for tea or coffee.

Pola   Did you get him here all right?

Jake   Yeah, no thanks to you.

Pola   How much longer are they going to be?

Jake   He hasn't even been seen by a doctor yet.

Pola   Shit.

Jake   They're still waiting.

Pola   She won't kick up enough fuss.

Jake   Well, why don't you go and raise merry hell?

Pola   He's not my boyfriend. I'm cold.

Jake   Come inside then.

Pola   No . . .

Jake   Still got some walls to tag out here?

Pola   I'd heard there's a newly whitewashed wall behind outpatients, but some bastard's beat me to it. There's not a single space on the brickwork. Sure, I could paint over some of the names already on there but it would look even more like shite than it does already. I hate crowded walls and I hate bloody amateurs who haven't sufficient imagination to use more than one colour. It's cowboys like them gives us vandals a bad name.

Jake   So how long've you just been standing around out here?

Pola   Standing around – me? There're some builders' skips round in the other car park – nice bit of virgin metalwork, untouched by pen, spray or airbrush. I tagged them, then I climbed up on one to see what was inside . . .

Jake   Dead patients?

Pola   No . . . phones, a couple of chairs, a cupboard unit, a pretty vase. I rescued all the good stuff, put it over the wall on to the waste ground. I'll come back for it tomorrow, shift it at a car-boot at the weekend.

Jake   You don't have a car.

Pola   I'll put the stuff out on a blanket.

Jake   You and Aimee are so different. The things you want out of life . . .

Pola   Did she tell you what she wants?

Jake   No . . .

Pola   She's never told me.

Pause.

Milk and three sugars, if you don't remember.

Jake   I want to talk to you.

Pola   You have, now piss off.

Jake   Is it over then, between us?

Pola   Over? Over – I like that! What did we ever have that could be over? What was there ever between *us*?

Jake *takes a bar of soap from his pocket, holds it out.*

Pola   Is it yours?

Jake   Fuck knows.

Jake *strokes* **Pola***'s face. They kiss.* **Pola** *pulls away.*

Pola   Jake . . .

Jake   What?

Pause.

What is it?

Pola   What?

Jake   What do you mean 'what'? You were going to say something.

Pola   Was I? Let me think . . .

Pause.

Just give me a second, OK. Got to collect my thoughts . . .

Pause.

Jake   I can hear the little cogs turning.

Pola   Kiss me.

Jake   That it?

Pola   I said . . .

Jake   I know.

He kisses her and they continue to get amorous. **Aimee** *gets up abruptly, starts pacing in front of* **Sam**.

Aimee (*angrily*)   What are you trying to do? Do to us, Sam?

Jake (*to* **Pola**)   That's good . . .

Aimee   You think this'll split us up?

Jake   Oh, that is good.

Aimee   Pola and me. Is that what you're trying to do? You want to ruin my life. You want to spoil everything, don't you? Now she's gone, I don't know where. I don't know if she'll come back, or whether she's disappeared again, and I might not see her for years. (*Quietly.*) I might never see my sister again. (*Louder, angrier.*) And it's all your fault! It was only a few flashing bulbs and some music. What's wrong with that? Why can't you be normal? Why can't you snap out of it?

Jake *and* **Pola** *merge into the shadows, making out against the wall. The sounds of their rough and passionate lovemaking accompany* **Aimee** *as she turns on* **Sam**.

Aim'ee   Snap out of it! Snap out of it! You bastard! Bastard. Oh, I hate you! I hate you. God, I hate you, Sam!!

Pola (*cries out*)   Aimeeeeee

Jake   Shit. What the . . .!

Jake *and* **Pola** *break apart, emerge from the shadows, adjusting their clothing.*

Pola   I thought . . . I thought I saw Aimee . . .

Jake   So what?

Pola   Fuck . . . Look, can you just leave me –

Jake   Right. Fine. But just let me tell you one thing. You're seriously fucked-up, sister . . .

Aimee   Pola?

She joins them.

Pola, you've come back. Are you OK? I thought I heard you scream.

Pola   It was just a rat crawled out of rubbish.

Aimee   You're cold and damp. Did Jake bring you a cup of tea?

Jake   I hadn't got as far as –

Pola   Tea with three sugars. No sugars for Aimee, she's dieting.

Aimee Thanks, Jake.

Exit **Jake**.

Aimee He's nice.

Pola He's a shit. Where's Sam?

Aimee Exactly where I left him. He can't come to much harm, but I can't make myself worry any more. I know this sounds awful, but if I'd sat there beside him any longer, I'd have ended up hitting him . . .

Pola So let's go hit him.

Aimee No . . .

Pola Or shout and scream and swear at him. That's what you should've done straight away. Get it off your chest. It won't hurt him and it'll make you feel better.

Aimee Why doesn't love last?

Pola It does, Aimee . . . if it was real to begin with.

Aimee Like you and Jake?

Pola Me and *who*?

Aimee You never change. Do you remember Dominic?

Pola Naturally. Blond, really into *The X-Files* and *Star Trek*, used to long for the good old days of *Blake's 7*.

Aimee I thought it was real with him. Until I saw him with you.

Pola I was testing him . . .

Aimee Did he pass with flying colours?

Pola He wasn't good enough. How could he be if he'd leave you for me?

Aimee I don't quite follow your reasoning.

Pola Never mind. He wasn't Mr Right. Agreed?

Aimee   For either of us. And you don't think Sam and
Jake –

Pola   And neither do you.

Aimee   Did you get a puppy?

Pola   They'd sold out. But I tagged some skips and a wall
in the car park. Over here.

Aimee *follows* **Pola** *to a tagged area of wall.*

Pola   I've still got to finish filling this one in.

She uses her spray can to fill in the letters of 'SISS' on the wall.

This is turning out to be one hell of a weekend, isn't it? I
wonder what tomorrow and Sunday have in store.

Aimee   Don't.

Pola   I knew we were in for trouble the moment I laid eyes
on Sam.

Aimee   I'd really wanted you and Sam to get on.

Pola   Sure.

Aimee   And since you both like art . . . I thought maybe
he could get you commissioned to paint a few pictures for
the apartments in the new complex in Famagusta.

Pola   Nice little watercolours of palm trees and street
cafés? (*Impersonating* **Sam**.) I don't think that's quite my bag.

She changes to another colour spray-paint.

I've thought up a tag for you.

She sprays 'AIM' on the wall.

You'll have to practise it. You always have to write it the
same, like your signature. Fast and accurate, that's the
secret.

Aimee   Give me the paint-spray.

Pola   Aimee! What will Sam think? Do you want to be a mindless vandal?

Aimee   I just want to try it.

Pola   You might find it easier to start with a marker pen.

Aimee   I want to make it big.

She draws a fat, wobbly 'A' on the wall.

I can't stop it going wobbly.

Pola   Get closer to the wall. You don't need to keep a lookout, that's what I'm here for.

Aimee   It's much harder than I would've thought.

Aimee *finishes her tag.*

Pola   You bet. Among the real street painters in New York and LA you don't get to call yourself an artist until you've spent at least three years honing your talents to perfection.

Aimee   Shall I do one for Sam?

Pola   How about this?

Pola *writes 'COMA'.*

Aimee   No! . . . you cow.

Pola   So what've you been doing in your almost-married life? Do you still go up the West End?

Aimee   No.

Pola   The Ministry of Sound?

Aimee   We don't go out much.

Pola   I suppose the only club Sam's into is a bridge club.

Aimee   We watch telly. He took me to see *Sense and Sensibility*.

Pola   No wonder Mother loves him so much. I bet she's already talking grandchildren.

Aimee   Yes . . . she is.

Pola   And she's already bought them their first healing crystals – blue for a boy, and pink for a girl.

Aimee   I must phone Mum about my crystal to find out for sure whether the damaged bit will affect its properties.

Pola   It's just a bloody lump of rock. It doesn't have 'properties'. How can it? Let Mother believe in that shit if she wants to. She's getting old, her life can only get worse from here on. Being old's a fuckin' grim deal. I don't blame her for clutching at straws. But don't you start believing in that stuff just yet.

Aimee   I wish you'd come and see her.

Pola   We'd only start rowing again. (*Beat.*) Pizza.

Aimee   What?

Pola   Shit, I'd forgotten all about it! I must be losing, *finally* losing my geraniums. Are you hungry?

Aimee   Yes, but –

Exit **Pola**.

Where are you . . . hey, Pola! Wait . . .

Exit **Aimee**.

Jake *rejoins* **Sam**.

Jake   Thought I might find you here, old man. The girls are still outside. I think I can safely say this is the weirdest evening I've ever spent. I know you're a man of the world, Sam. You've been here, there and everywhere, but are there women as strange as those two all over the world, or is it something peculiar to Sydenham?

Not got a fag on you, by any chance? I'd given up, but all of this is enough to make anyone . . .

He rummages in **Sam**'s *pockets, finds his wallet, takes out his credit cards.*

You've enough cards to play poker with. And a donor card? Who'd want a bit of you, for fuck's sake?

He discovers **Sam**'s *wallet contains a lot of banknotes.*

Only joking, mate. You're not short of cash, are you? I don't suppose you could . . .

He pockets **Sam**'s *wallet.*

I'm only borrowing it, all right, Sammy?

He talks to **Sam** *without looking at him.*

I'll pay you back one day. Don't lose sleep over it. You know, the thing I've noticed about you blokes with an impressive income – you never spend it. You don't know how to live. I hope you don't mind me talking to you like this, but you strike me as a guy who doesn't know how to live.

Sam *twitches slightly, lifts his head slowly and turns it to look at* **Jake**, *who talks on, oblivious.*

Jake   You've got a great job, money, travel, everything . . . what you need to do is chill out and enjoy it. Take some time off, let Aimee take you out to meet some new people, try some things you've been telling yourself you're too old for, or 'aren't quite your thing' –

He looks at **Sam**. **Sam**'s *hand jerks out at* **Jake** *as if he is asking for his money back.*

Shit . . . !

Sam *splutters and coughs. He tries to shield his eyes from the light with his arm and his jacket. His speech is slurred but coherent.*

Sam   Lights off. Turn the lights off!

Jake   All right . . . all right, mate.

Jake *looks around for a light switch.*

Sam Turn the music off.

Jake Music? There isn't any music.

Suddenly, **Sam** *grabs hold of* **Jake**.

Jake Fucking Jesus Christ!

They fall struggling on to the floor.

Sam Money. Give me my money!

Shaken, **Jake** *frees himself. He takes* **Sam**'s *wallet from his pocket and throws it back to him.*

Jake I just thought it might be better if I looked after it for a while . . . well, hospitals, you don't know who you can trust. I'll, I'll go and find a doctor.

Exit **Jake**.

Blackout.

Scene Two

Outside the hospital. **Sam** *traces with his finger the outline of* **Pola**'s *SISS tag on the wall.* **Jake** *watches.*

Sam Corn-baked yellow . . . hot sun . . . Sunshine poem, sunshine song.

Jake A right pillock you made me look. Two doctors and three nurses. 'I left him right here,' I said. 'He can't be far away.'

Sam Furry bees . . . Gleaming bottles . . . Cast soft rainbows on the wall.

Jake Yeah, look you can't just hang around here all night . . .

Sam Dappled sunspots . . . Sunshine melting . . . Turns the sea florid crimson. Smelling salts!

Jake Er . . . are you feeling weird again?

Sam *remains looking at the lettering on the wall. He traces the word 'COMA' on the wall.*

Sam   Mindless . . . mindless . . . vandalism.

Jake   Right . . . Look, you'd better come back inside. Just get them to check you over.

Sam   This shell's from Madagascar.

Jake   Is it?

Sam   You know what I like about you? You're a good listener.

Jake   Yes, well . . . look, why don't we go for a drink or something, eh?

Sam *walks away unsteadily.*

Jake   Pub's this way.

Sam *ignores* **Jake**.

Jake   Hey . . . hey, where are you going?

Jake *blocks* **Sam**'s *way, tries to steady him.*

Sam   Get your hands off me!

Jake   All right, all right.

Sam   What are you? What kind of man are you? You're like them. Just the same as them . . . I heard you. I heard them. Get out of my way!

Jake   All right then. Right . . . OK, you're on your own, mate.

Exit **Jake**.

Sam *leans against the wall, traces the word 'AIM' with his finger.*

Enter **Pola** *and* **Aimee** *at the arcade. A pizza box is outside, beside the boat.*

Pola   There it is – cheese and tomato.

Aimee   What surprises me is that they still left it though no one was here to pay.

Pola   Ahh, you see Ricky knows me. (*Beat.*) And owes me.

Aimee   Have you one of his soaps?

Pause.

We mustn't leave Jake and Sam just sitting there for too long.

Pola   What harm can come to them? You're really becoming a worrier . . .

Aimee   Just like Mum?

Pola   No. I wasn't going to say that. (*Beat.*) Though come to think of it . . .

Aimee   What?

Pola *tilts* **Aimee**'s *face to look at her.*

Pola   No, it's OK.

Aimee   What? What's OK?

Pola   This afternoon, when you arrived, I thought you looked older.

Aimee   I am. A year older.

Pola   I thought you were starting to look like Mother.

Aimee   Charming.

Pola   But you've lost that 'old' look now . . .

Aimee   I'm glad to hear it. It probably *was* that chipped crystal. I was probably right to throw it in the sea, do you think?

Pola   Probably.

Pola *and* **Aimee** *sit side by side in* **Jake**'s *boat, eating pizza.*

Aimee   Pizza under the stars. Cheese is a bit rubbery.

Pola   It's supposed to be, Aimee.

Aimee   If they can't find a cure for Sam . . .

Pola   You make him sound like a disease.

Aimee   I'll have to stay here for a while longer . . .

Pola   They might take him to another hospital.

Aimee   They might, I suppose. It's funny, in a way what's happened has made my decision for me. Or rather, it's left me with no decision to make. I can't even think about leaving him now, can I?

Pola   I don't understand you. Why do you want to be with someone who's sick, Aimee?

Aimee   I don't but –

Pola   He might never recover. You might spend the rest of your life sitting beside a hospital bed, engaged to a vegetable. Is that what you want? Even if he does come out of it, you'll have to spend all your time watching and worrying in case it happens again. You'll spend a very boring life together, you and Sam. No lights, no music. But maybe you've changed, maybe that is what you really want now.

Aimee   No! (*Beat.*) I don't want to marry Sam.

Pola   So what *do* you want to do, Aimee?

Aimee   How do I know you won't leave me again? That you're not just telling me to leave Sam because you hate him?

Pola   I don't hate Sam. I do care what happens . . .

Aimee   Liar. You called a pizza when you said you were dialling 999. A pizza. That's a good substitute for an ambulance, Pola. That's very caring.

Pola   You promised me you'd never go away.

Aimee   *You* went away!

Pola I had to.

Aimee Oh sure. Just a stupid quarrel with Mum. That's all it took.

Pola I didn't leave because of Mother. I'd put up with her for years – fussing, interfering, trying to find me jobs, trying to make me keep them, trying to get me into college, trying to keep me sectioned . . .

Aimee She thought it was for the best. She was worried you'd try something stupid again . . . and I was worried too –

Pola I'm trying to explain. I left because I wanted to give you a chance.

Aimee What do you mean –

Pola A chance to grow. All our lives I've made all the fucking choices, you've just been along for the ride. That was fine when we were kids, Big Sis and Little Sis, but as we got older where did that leave you? When I came out of hospital the last time, I asked you what you'd been doing, who'd you been seeing – I wanted to catch up on the gossip. You'd done nothing but sit in our room! You'd done nothing without me. I knew then I get out of your life. I must give you a chance to make something of yourself, to find a job that makes you happy, someone who makes you happy.

Aimee I thought I had.

Pola You fucked up. I'd been gone, what, a month and you had to leave your job –

Aimee The boss assaulted me –

Pola You couldn't deal with it –

Aimee I didn't need to.

Pola So you went to work for Sam. You let him think you were in love with him.

Aimee I was. (*Beat.*) I thought I was.

Pola   You thought you were.

Aimee   I was lonely. I'd always hung out with you . . . and your friends –

Pola   When I had any. So I'm to blame for everything as usual. Fine.

Pola *turns her back on* **Aimee***, goes back into the arcade.*

Aimee   Pola!

She follows **Pola** *into the arcade.* **Pola** *is sorting her pens and paints and putting them in her bag.* **Aimee** *is in tears.*

Pola . . . Pola . . . if I live in your shadow, it's because that's where I want to be . . . People used to say, 'You mustn't live in your big sister's shadow, you must break out and do something for yourself.' The trouble is when I do it's not nearly as much fun. It's like living my life in black and white . . . I need you to colour it in.

Maybe some people are meant to grow up and grow apart . . . and others are mean to grow closer.

Pola   Every day I've imagined you here with me. Every time I've tagged a train, a signal box or a wall between here and Brighton. My tag's not just my identity. It's us both, Sis. We've taken evening walks along by the tracks, we've caught late-night trains and left our mark above their doors and windows. We've clambered up under motorway bridges and autographed signs pointing to all points of the compass. Every day, thousands of drivers and passengers see our tag, Sis . . .

Aimee   I wish I'd really been with you . . .

Pola   Trashing public transport? Being one of Sam's 'mindless vandals'?

Aimee   Just travelling around . . . leaving our mark in some way. Oh, my head's spinning. I need to get away. I need to escape.

Pola   From me? From Sam?

Aimee   Oh, I don't know . . . from Sam of course! From Sam. Help me! Pola, help me.

Pola   So let's escape . . .

She scrambles in the boat.

We'll take Jake's boat! We'll travel together. We'll live under the stars . . . or sleep in beach huts and caves if it's rainy. Collect up your clothes . . . no . . . just come in that dress . . .

Aimee   Now we've both got on our holiday dresses.

Pola   Yeah, mine's full of moth-holes.

She runs into the arcade, grabs some provisions – mugs, hats, guitar, other assorted clutter. **Aimee** *follows her example. They empty it all into the boat.*

We'll get a dog. You can name him . . . or her. We could get a cat too – a real ship's cat with sea legs. We better take the rest of the pizza for provisions. I can busk in pubs and cafés –

Aimee   – I can sing.

Pola   You can write all our songs – just put tunes to some of your poems. We'll build a camp in a tree, and collect firewood . . . We'll get marshmallows and toast them on twigs. I'll teach you how to nick from shops, so you'll never ever get caught. We can scrump apples, and vegetables from gardens. You'll write, I'll paint –

Aimee   – And you'll teach me to tag properly!

Pola *scrambles up on to the bow of the boat.*

Pola   We'll be a team. We'll be the best, we'll be legendary as tag artists – AIM and SISS!

Aimee *joins her.*

Aimee   AIM and SISS!

Pause.

Pola . . . I'd better pop back to the hospital, just to make sure Sam's being taken care of.

Pola *stops, looks at* **Aimee**.

Aimee   Then we can go! Oh, it's going to be brilliant. It'll be like before you went away. It'll be better! I won't be long. Is there anything you want me to buy . . . for provisions, on my way back?

Pola (*almost wearily*)   No, Aimee.

Exit **Aimee**.

Pola *goes back inside the arcade. She collects up the soap bars in her dress, takes them outside, scatters them on the shingle. She goes back inside and sits down on the floor of the arcade.*

Enter **Sam**. *He pauses for a moment, holding on to the side of the boat, still not totally coordinated. He staggers into the arcade, startling* **Pola**.

Sam   Tell me your secret! Tell me your fucking secret!

Pola   Sam!

She laughs.

Oh my God.

Sam (*more quietly*)   Where's Aimee?

Pola *shrugs.*

Sam   Where is Aimee?

Pola   I preferred you when you were in a coma.

Sam   Where's she gone? She hates me, doesn't she? How did you do that?

Pola   Get away from me.

Sam   How did you make her hate me? How did you do it?

Pola   I didn't. You did it.

Sam   You don't love her. You don't want her.

Pola   You haven't a clue what I want.

Sam   You don't really love her.

Pola   Love, Sam? Love? I thought all you knew about was money, money, money. How much were those sandwiches?

Sam   What have I done to you? What have I taken from you?

Pola   Nothing. Nothing at all. I've won, Sam. Aimee wants to stay with me. I've won.

Sam *grabs hold of* **Pola**, *stumbling, pulling them both down on the floor.*

Pola (*panicky*)   Get off!

Sam   You've won, have you?

Pola   Fucking get off me!

Sam *holds* **Pola** *down.*

Sam   Just you listen to me. I want to talk to you.

Pola   Fuck you.

Sam   As soon as I met you, I could feel what you were doing. Little by little, bit by bit, you were tearing her from me. Ripping my Aimee from my arms.

Sam *puts his hands around her throat.*

Pola   *My* Aimee. Ow, you're hurting me!

Sam   I could feel the anger building up inside me, the anger and fear. My nerves, my muscles, the veins inside my head felt like they were stretching, and swelling. Swelling until they were about to burst . . .

Sam *is choking* **Pola**. *She gasps for breath.*

Pola   You should get a crystal, Sam. They're very calming.

Sam   You laugh at me, but are you happy, Pola? Are you happy now?

Pola   Yes, Sam. I'm happy.

Pola *laughs, but her laugh is painful, bordering on hysteria.* **Sam** *releases her. He stays on the floor beside her.*

Sam   I don't think you're happy. I think you're a sad and lonely little girl, saying 'Look at me! look at me! aren't I clever! I've won, I've won!'

Pola   I want you to leave. I want you to go right now.

Pola *sits up slowly.* **Sam** *sits up. Slowly, he touches her hair, her face.*

Sam   You see, I loved Aimee for herself, for being Aimee . . . not just as someone to stand back and admire *me*. Not just as someone to listen to *me*, to laugh at *my* jokes, to keep reassuring *me* about how clever I am, and how much fun I'm having.

Pola   But *you're* not clever, Sam, even though you think you are. And when was the last time you actually had some fun? (*Beat.*) What? Can't you remember?

Pause.

Not had much fun lately, have you?

Sam   I'm not the only one. Tell me you're happy, Pola. Look me in the eye and tell me.

Pola *turns her head to look him in the eye.*

Pola   Piss off.

Pause.

I was happy before you came back to life. I'll be happy when you're out of here. Go on, get out.

Sam *goes to his suitcase.*

Pola   Yeah, and take your old crap with you.

Sam   I know you're not happy. I don't think you're
capable of happiness . . . because you don't really care about
anyone or anything – do you?

Sam *takes a bar of soap from his washbag, inside the suitcase.*

Pola   Hark at you, Doctor Sam. You come out of a
fucking coma and you think that makes you know it all.
Well, let me tell you this – you're still the same smug,
superior bastard you were before. That's why my sister's left
you. It's not because of me.

Sam *picks up the case.*

Pola   I've done you a fucking favour, mate. One day you'll
see that.

Sam *makes to leave the arcade. Passing* **Pola***, he pushes his bar of
soap into her hands. She clasps his hand.*

Sam   Add that to your collection.

Sam *pulls his hand free, leaving* **Pola** *holding the soap.*

Exit **Sam***.*

Pola *lies down on the floor of the arcade, looking at the soap.*

Enter **Aimee***.*

Aimee   Pola, guess what? He'd gone! A nurse said she'd
seen him leave the hospital. Can you believe it? Sam's
better! I don't have to worry about him any more. There's
nothing to stop us leaving now.

Jake had gone too . . . Oh God, he might be heading back
here! If we're going to take the boat we better go quickly.
Come on, get up.

She drags **Pola** *to her feet.* **Pola** *stands looking at* **Sam***'s soap.*

Have you packed everything? All our supplies? What've you
got . . .

She sees the soap.

Sam's . . . (*She stops herself.*) The bag with your paints, mustn't forget that . . .

She puts the bag of paints over **Pola**'s *shoulder.* **Aimee** *collects up* **Pola**'s *sunglasses.*

And your sunglasses . . . which pair do you want to wear? These? The funky ones?

She puts the sunglasses on top of **Pola**'s *head.*

Come on.

She puts an arm around the still silent and subdued **Pola** *and leads her to the boat.*

Let's go and tag every lighthouse around the coast!

Aimee *picks up one end of the boat. After a moment,* **Pola** *picks up the other.*

Exit **Pola** *and* **Aimee** *carrying the boat.*

Blackout.

People on the River

People on the River was first performed at the Red Room, the Finborough, London, on 27 May 1997. The cast was as follows:

Phil	Benedict Martin
Louise	Kate Wilton
Marina	Kate Elizabeth Ricketts
Nicky	Daniel Harcourt
Evan	Tom Bushe
Elsa	Jackie Everett
Singing Telegram	
Justine	
Stylist	Elaine Pyke
DJ	
David	
Greg	
Guido	David Eastman
Harassed Person	
Roslyn	Christina Greatrex
Andrew Morton	As himself

Directed by Lisa Goldman
Designed by Alastair Galbraith
Costumes by Elaine White
Lighting by Aideen Malone
Sound by Rueben Garrett
Music by John Evans
Fights Kevin Murphy
Assistant Director Alison Newman

Act One

Scene One

A full-length curtain lines the back of the stage. Under dim lighting,
Louise *sits on one of several padded seats set in a semicircle. On a
small table in front of her is a jug of water, some plastic cups and a
jotter. All kinds of cables cross the floor. On a wall back, is a video
screen.* **Louise** *holds her hands tightly in her lap, as if worried they'll
run away. Suddenly a blinding light illuminates* **Louise**. *She starts
and looks round.*

Enter **Phil**, *the floor manager.*

Phil   Could you face front please. We're just adjusting
your personal lighting.

Louise *faces front again.*

Phil   OK, can you just say something? I need to check the
levels.

Louise   What do you want me to –?

Phil (*interrupting*)   Cool.

Enter **Marina**, *a TV presenter. She offers* **Louise** *a professional
smile.*

Marina   It's a very hectic day here today, Louise.

She sits down beside **Louise**.

I'm still not happy about the mike . . . Andrew said he'd
look at it . . .

Phil   Let's have a look then . . .

Phil *leans over* **Marina** *to adjust her personal microphone.*

Marina   New shirt?

Phil   Yeah.

Marina   You see – I do notice. OK, that's enough, move.

Phil *moves back.*

Phil　Try that.

Marina　One, two, three, four.

Phil　Fine.

Exit **Phil**.

Marina *gets a message in her earpiece.*

Marina　Right . . . (*To* **Louise**.) I think we're about ready to go. Are we? . . . We're ready now? Right.

Music plays. **Marina** *steps forward and is immediately flooded in light.*

(*Directly to us.*) Good evening and welcome. On the show tonight, I'll be talking to Professor Caroline Mottram about her new book which claims your pet cat could have telepathic powers. You'll have an exclusive chance to sample the new single from Tarelle James. And I'll be taking a look at the latest crop of Hollywood releases. But first cast your minds back to September of last year . . . when we saw the young widow of a hit-and-run victim make this emotional plea.

The video screen flickers into life. On screen we see **Louise**, *looking tired and haggard, sitting behind a table at a press conference. Around her, reporters jostle, flashes flash.*

Louise (*on-screen*)　*All I want to say is . . . if the . . . the person who did this is out there watching this now . . . please, whoever you are, for God's sake, come forward . . .*

Marina　Now, tonight four months later, I'm pleased to welcome Louise Fielder on to the show.

Louise *hesitates.*

Louise　Hello.

Marina　It must have been very hard for you these past months . . .

Louise   Very. On the whole family. We've just been trying to take each day as it comes . . . but it doesn't seem to be getting any easier. I only need to hear a car horn or screech of brakes outside and I go cold . . .

Marina *nods in sympathy.*

Marina   It brings it all back?

Louise   It never goes away.

Marina   What were your feelings, Louise, when you heard on the news, that in response to your appeal, someone had turned themselves in at your local police station?

Louise   Well, relief in a way . . . it helped to know that the . . . the person who did this, had some . . . feeling even if, for whatever reason, he couldn't stop for even a moment to see what he'd done . . .

Marina   And with the understandable hurt and anger you feel towards the man who caused your heartache, are you now able to look in your heart and find some forgiveness towards –

Louise (*interrupting*)   It's too early to talk of forgiving . . .

Marina   Yet, you have agreed on this programme to meet Nicky Farrell, the man who was driving the car which failed to stop after hitting and fatally injuring your husband . . . Could you join us now please, Nicky.

Enter **Nicky**.

Marina *and then* **Louise** *stand up.* **Nicky** *shakes* **Marina**'*s hand. They all sit down again.*

Marina   Nicky, hallo and welcome to the programme. It must be a very difficult thing to come here today . . .

Nicky *looks at* **Louise**. *She glares back.*

Marina   That evening when you saw Louise's appeal on your TV screen –

Nicky I didn't see the film . . .

Marina What?

Nicky I didn't see her . . . on the telly.

Marina But earlier you said . . . (*She stops herself.*)

Nicky First I saw of it was on your monitor back there just now.

Marina So then how did you –

Nicky One of my friends told me about it.

Marina And you'd already confessed to him . . .

Nicky Her. Yeah, we went for a drink, cos I was really shook up, right? She didn't know what was up with me, cos I was shaking and talking really fast. She thought I was speeding or something . . .

Marina When it happened? You *were* speeding, weren't you?

Nicky What? No, I was clean.

Marina I mean you were travelling too fast.

Nicky I didn't know that at the time. I mean, I was surprised when they told me what I'd been doing.

Louise Eighty miles an hour in a built-up area! A street where *children* play!

Marina We'll come back to you in a minute, Louise. (*To* **Nicky**.) So you confessed to your friend, and then *she* saw Louise's appeal on the TV?

Nicky Yeah. When we were in the pub, and I told her what I'd done, she didn't believe me. She just thought I was completely off my face and rushing away with myself . . .

Nicky *leans forward, rips a page from the jotter. He sits back and starts folding it.*

Marina OK . . . so then you decided to give yourself up?

Nicky Yeah . . . more or less . . .

Marina Why?

Louise (*mutters*) So they'd let him off . . .

Nicky Didn't have much choice . . . I knew they were sure to find out sooner or later. And I felt bad about it. I mean, I didn't want people to think I didn't care that I'd hit somebody. I did. I was really cut up about it. It stopped me sleeping and everything.

Louise It stopped you *sleeping*?

Marina But when it happened. When you knew your car had hit someone – you didn't stop.

Louise Yes, why didn't you stop!

Marina Can you recall the thoughts that were running through your head, Nicky?

Nicky I did stop. Saw the bloke just lying there. Saw some people come out of a shop to take care of him. Once I knew he was being taken care of, then I drove off.

Louise Why?

Marina Why, Nicky. Why did you drive off?

Nicky I needed to clean the car.

Louise *gasps, shakes her head.* **Marina** *looks at her.*

Louise (*softly*) Bastard.

Marina You cleaned the car so no one would know you'd hit somebody?

Louise (*to* **Nicky**) You're sick . . .

Nicky Clean the car *inside*. Make sure there was nothing on the floor there shouldn't have been.

Louise He's off his head. He's on drugs or something.

Nicky I should be so lucky.

Louise   You *are* lucky! You're still alive, unlike my husband.

Marina   Let's try and discuss this calmly.

Louise   You got off with a poxy suspended sentence!

Nicky   And a three-month driving ban.

Louise   My Darren's dead!

Marina   To take us back to the day in question. (*Pause.*) Had you been taking drugs?

Nicky   Me?

Louise   Yeah, you – forever trying to dodge responsibility.

Nicky   Hey, I'm not dodging anything . . . though I wish I had dodged your old man . . . I owned up I did it. I'm here now.

Louise   Are they paying you?

Nicky   No. Are they paying you?

Marina   Let's get back to the subject in question. Nicky . . . at the time you ran down and killed Darren Fielder were you under the influence of any . . . any illegal substances?

Nicky   It was a *Monday afternoon*. I don't know anyone who's under the influence of *anything* on a Monday. I mean, Monday's a day of the dead . . . (*Pause.*) Can you cut that line? I mean, with Mr Fielder being dead and everything.

Marina   It's a live show . . .

Louise   You can't hurt me any more. Nothing you can say can hurt me.

Nicky *sets his finished origami figure down on the table.*

Nicky   Nobody's trying to hurt you. I don't want to hurt you, Louise.

Louise   Don't you think killing my husband hurt me? You can't possibly know how I feel . . .

Nicky *rips another piece of paper from the jotter.*

Nicky   If someone had killed a member of my family . . . even by accident . . . I couldn't forgive them. I'd want to kill them.

Louise   You don't know what it feels like.

Nicky   Well, I'd probably go round and beat them up . . . at the very least. So I can understand Louise's anger.

Louise   Your understanding won't bring my Darren back. It won't pay my debts . . .

Marina   OK, right . . . So where's the future, Louise?

Louise   Just taking each day as it comes, I suppose. I can't really plan or think ahead at all. Not yet. Darren and me had planned everything together. We were buying a house, we were both working. Now I can't work, and I'm losing the house. I'm back living with my mum/

Marina   /Who's here in the audience tonight.

Lights pick out **Elsa** *among the theatre audience. She isn't sure whether to wave. She starts to, then wishes she hadn't.*

Louise   /Eventually, I'm hoping to start a group to offer help, advice and a listening ear to people who've been bereaved in a similar way . . .

Marina   So something positive, however small, might come out of this terribly tragic experience. And Nicky? What are your plans for the future?

Nicky   I want to somehow put all of this behind me/

Louise   Easy for you!/

Nicky   /and get out and do something . . . like get some more gigs for my band . . .

Marina   Yes, Nicky Farrell and his friend Evan have recently formed a pop band called Alice Don't Surf . . . and he has a surprise for you, Louise. Do you want to tell her about it, Nicky?

Nicky *leans forward to look at* **Louise** *properly*.

Nicky   Louise, I've written you a song . . . to try to put into words how sorry I am about killing your husband.

Marina   And Nicky and Evan are going to perform it especially for you, Louise. Live on this show.

Enter **Evan** *in army fatigues with his guitar*. **Nicky** *joins him*.

Marina *stands to introduce them*.

Marina   Alice Don't Surf, with their song, 'Hit And Run'.

Nicky *and* **Evan** *play the song*.

Tonight when I'm speeding I see you
At the moment I lose control
Braking, braking as time stands still
The shock on your face, then you're gone
Then you're gone.

Hit and run, I'm speeding away
Hit and run, I was taken today
Running from the horror and fear that's still to come.

You're sprawled on the tarmac, smashed and torn
But I'm dead inside, can't face what I've done
As your life blood bleeds slowly away
My foot slams back down hard to the floor.

Hit and run, I'm speeding away
Hit and run, you were taken today
Running from the nightmare and the guilt that's still to come.

Gonna drive this death machine tonight
Burning rubber, and petrol, and chrome
Take a last, fuel-injected hit
To escape from this wreckage, this life
This wreckage, this life.

Hit and run, I'm speeding away
Hit and run, you took me today
Running from the anger and sorrow that's still to come
Still to come (*repeat and fade*).

Louise *watches in disbelief.* **Phil** *comes back in, stands beside* **Marina** *to watch the band.* **Louise** *gets up, runs off the stage.* **Elsa** *gets up out of the audience, looking back angrily at the people who were sitting behind her. She follows* **Louise** *off. At the end of the song* **Phil** *goes up to* **Nicky** *and* **Evan**.

Phil   That was great, guys . . .

Exit **Phil** *with* **Nicky** *and* **Evan**.

Enter **Louise** *and* **Elsa**, *wandering back across the stage looking at an A–Z.*

Elsa   People tutted when I got up out of the audience . . . just cos I was blotting out their view of that man's band for a few seconds. So rude. There's no manners these days. I started explaining to one woman. 'That's my youngest daughter up there, that was my son-in-law that yobbo killed.' And she had the nerve to shush me. How I didn't take a swipe at her . . .

Louise   How could he . . . that bastard . . . sing that song about *my* Darren. How could he!

Elsa   You know, I didn't take to that Marina woman, not at all. She seems rather *artificial*. Not real. Not with any understanding, like someone like Oprah or Vanessa has, for example . . .

Louise   Why didn't she let me speak! She wouldn't let me talk about Darren. I tried to . . . I tried . . .

Enter **Marina** *with a pile of papers.*

Marina   Louise, Elsa, glad I've caught you. Just look what I've got here! You really touched a nerve with the viewers. Lots of warmth, and messages of support flowing in for you already. Let me read you some of these faxes.

She holds a floppy fax paper letter up to read it.

'Dear Louise, I thought I'd fax let you know that some of us do really know what you're currently going through. Our beloved son was killed by joyriders, five years ago. They were never caught and the pain is with me every single day of my life. Your idea of starting a self-help group is a good one. At first people were very kind, but after a while friends tire of hearing about it, and you do still need to talk . . . and have someone there to listen . . .'

I'll let you read the rest yourself. She gives her address, so when you get the group started, perhaps you'll be able to reach out.

She turns to another letter.

Oh, er . . . This one's a marriage proposal . . . you always get a few weirdos – statistically there's lots of them out there. He's even faxed you his photo, look.

Elsa takes the letter from **Marina**.

Elsa   He doesn't look weird. I wish more young men still had marriage on their minds. (*Looking at the letter.*) Oh, and he says he's a Christian.

Marina   We had a call from the features editor of *Just Woman*. She's very keen to talk to you.

Elsa   Does she pay/

Marina   /I happen to know her personally, and she's a very *warm*, very supportive woman.

She checks her watch.

Look, I must go, got the usual post-prod debriefings. But do keep in touch, Louise. Let us know when you get the support group off the ground. We might possibly be able to do a follow-up piece. You never know. Well . . . it was a privilege to meet the both of you. Take care. Safe journey.

Blackout.

Scene Two

Front of stage, **Nicky** *sits on the floor writing in a jotter.* **Evan** *is practising chords on his rifle as if it was a guitar.* **Nicky** *rips up the page he has been writing on.*

Nicky   Shit.

Evan *takes off his headphones.*

Evan   Still not happening?

Nicky   No.

Evan   How do you think Simon and Garfunkel did it?

Nicky   Fuck knows. Fetch your guitar.

Evan *fetches his guitar.*

Nicky   Just strum it.

Evan *strums the guitar.*

Evan   If you could give me an opening line I could come up with a tune.

Nicky   If you could give me a tune, I could get some shit-hot words to it straight off.

Evan *plays a couple of bars.*

Nicky   Yeah . . . No, it's someone else's.

Pause.

We could buy *The Beatles Songbook* . . . just alter the tunes a bit . . .

Evan   I think it's been done, mate.

Nicky   Well, everything's ripped off from somewhere, isn't it?

Evan   Do you think that guy Phil is serious about being able to get us some top gigs?

Nicky   He seemed to know his stuff. And if he can get us on at the Mean Fiddler . . .

Evan   We should've grilled him a bit more before we said he could be our manager though – find out whether he's really got all these contacts in the business, or if he's just a bullshitter. What did he say he does at the TV studio?

Nicky   He's a floor manager.

Evan   He manages floors?

Nicky   He was right about the record companies picking up on our TV appearance. I'm not so sure he's right about signing with the biggest label though . . . I quite fancy going with a smaller indie company.

Evan   Shit, Nicky, let's go with the one putting the most on the table. We might never be in this kind of position again. It's fucking dreamtime, isn't it? This time last week we couldn't get anyone to listen to our demo, and now we've three companies clamouring to sign us.

Nicky   One farewell gig in Littlehampton's finest boozer and it's off to the bright lights for Alice.

Evan   So how many songs did you tell this manager we've got?

Nicky   Twelve. Enough for our first album, I thought, like.

Evan   Good thinking. And how many do we actually have?

Nicky   Two. And a title.

Evan   Shit. You said you were going to write some more last night.

Nicky   It didn't happen.

Evan   You couldn't be arsed?

Nicky   I didn't feel inspired . . . I mean, I just kept seeing her face . . . on that show, the way she looked at me . . .

Evan   You've got to forget that now. You've got to rise above it.

Nicky   How can I rise above it, Evan? All I can think about is her . . . and Darren Fielder . . . what kind of person he was . . .

Evan   It's no good thinking about what he was. He ain't any more. Time to move on. You've got to see this thing as a journey . . . You've been through it and come out the other side. You can rise from the ashes and be strong.

Nicky   I don't feel strong.

Evan   You've gotta be. This is our big chance. We've already got 'Hit and Run' and 'Killing A Dream'.

Nicky   See, I could write those because they were about something that had happened to me. But I can't keep having car accidents to give me something to write about.

Evan   You just need to think about something else that's happened.

Nicky   Nothing else has happened to me. I haven't been out in weeks.

Evan   Write about that. Use your pain, the nightmares. Darkness and death.

Nicky   I want to get away from all of that.

Evan   We need ten more songs by the end of the week.

Nicky   I know . . . and I can only think of the blood . . . the blood in the road.

Evan   Blood in the road.

Nicky (*resignedly*)   That's another title.

Nicky *writes it down.* **Evan** *strums the guitar.*

Evan   By the way, I *was* serious about what I said earlier.

Nicky   And I don't think it's such a good idea, that's all. I mean, we'd all agreed on the image thing . . . if you wear army uniform it'll look out of place.

Evan   Like I'm an outsider.

Nicky   Yeah.

Evan   Well, I will be, prowling around with my guitar . . .

Evan *demonstrates.*

Nicky   Like some blown-away veteran of the Vietnam war . . .

Evan   Yeah!

Nicky   Yeah, it's nice, Evan, but it doesn't fit in with the music, the image. I just think the balaclava and the rifle are . . . I don't know, they look a bit camp . . . even though you're not, of course you're not, don't let's start on that one.

Evan   I'm not saying I'll always wear combats, like. Just for a while, just while I'm making my protest.

Nicky   I can't see how seeing you on *Top of the Pops* is going to make anyone at the MOD have second thoughts about the results of your psychological profile.

Evan   But I passed all the physical tests and everything.

Nicky   Yeah, you were in the paras for a day. No one'll ever be able to take that away from you.

The doorbell rings.

Evan   And I'll wear my uniform with pride. I'd have been a fucking amazing paratrooper. Let the army see what they've lost by their fucking psychological profiling.

The doorbell rings again.

Shall I get that if you're busy composing?

Exit **Evan.**

Nicky   Blood on the road . . . death on my mind . . .

Enter **Evan** *with a* **Singing Telegram** *carrying a ribbon-wrapped box.*

Singing Telegram   Are you Nicky Farrell?

(*Sings.*) Here's a little song to say
Hope you have a very special day
I'm making someone's dream come true
By bringing this gift especially for you.

Singing Telegram *hands* **Nicky** *the present and exits.*

Nicky   Maybe it's from one of the record companies . . .

He opens the box. He recoils.

Fucking hell!

Blackout.

Scene Three

Elsa *and* **Louise** *are sitting with a man,* **David**. *The atmosphere is rather tense.*

Louise   I think what I'm saying is the reason we're here is to share our pain . . . to try to ease our grief a little by talking about our experiences. Do you want to start, David? Maybe talk a little bit about how you're feeling.

Pause.

Or perhaps I should say something first . . .

Elsa   Go on, dear.

Louise   OK . . . I'm starting this group to help me deal with losing my husband Darren . . . nearly four months ago . . . We'd only been married for six months . . . though we'd known each other for a couple of years . . . I can't describe how I felt . . . I mean, when a policeman rang the doorbell and told me he'd been involved in an accident . . . You think you're with someone, they'll always be there.

She pauses. **David** *nods.*

You know how it is . . . You can't believe, all of a sudden your everything's been taken from you . . . Sometimes I just hear someone laugh . . . and I look round thinking it must be him. And when I hear a song on the radio . . . I mean, like a week before the accident we were papering our kitchen, and he was singing along with the radio – 'You're the One that I Want' – from *Grease* . . . Darren slicks his hair back with the wallpaper paste . . . doing a John Travolta . . . Course, his hair sets hard . . . and we spend the rest of the night trying to wash it out . . . I'm sorry . . . He was my best friend . . . and I wasn't there when he died . . . wasn't there . . .

Exit **Louise**.

An awkward pause.

David　John Travolta . . . now he's a nice bloke. Very down-to-earth in real life . . . despite the Scientology thing . . .

Elsa　You've met John Travolta?

David　Only the once. He was over here to talk to Barry Norman, so you know, I got introduced.

Elsa　You know Barry Norman? I always think he looks like a nice man.

David　He is, yeah.

Elsa　So what, he's a friend of yours or do you work in telly or something?

David　I just work behind the scenes . . . doing research mainly . . .

Elsa　You must meet some interesting people.

David　Well, it depends what show I'm working on.

Elsa So what shows have you –

David *Wogan, Jonathan Ross* – I did all the research on their guests and that. Lately, I've been on *Wish You Were Here* . . .

Elsa It's not true about Judith Chalmers, is it?

David I'm afraid it is.

Pause.

Anthea's terrific though . . . very professional, and a really nice person.

Elsa You know her too? And I suppose you know Marina Walker.

David I saw you and your daughter on the show.

Elsa I didn't warm to Marina . . . She should never have let that lout on there.

David It's funny, I was discussing it with Esther and she said exactly the same thing.

Elsa Esther Rantzen?

David Lovely lady. Lovely smile. Esther said she wished Louise had been on her show instead.

Elsa I wish she had been too. I'm sure Esther would've let her talk about Darren and promote this group.

David She'd have been marvellous. You know . . . I suppose I could always still have a word. With Esther. If Louise and you would be interested in appearing on her show.

The doorbell rings.

Elsa Oh we would, yes. (*Calls.*) Louise, someone at the door. (*To* **David**.) If you are going to be speaking to Esther and you do get the chance to mention it . . .

David   What's the time? (*He checks his watch.*) We might just catch her.

He switches the TV on. **Esther** *is on.* **David** *sits forward and starts addressing the TV.* **Elsa** *flinches, looks like she wants to move away from him.*

Esther . . . Esther, it's David . . . Yeah, I'm fine. Look, I don't know if this is a bad time, but I've some people here who'd like to be on the show . . .

Enter **Louise** *with* **Roslyn** *(a smartly dressed businesswoman).*

You will? That's great, Esther.

Louise   Mum . . . David, this is Roslyn.

David   Hi.

David *offers* **Roslyn** *his hand.* **Roslyn** *shakes it and sits down.*

Louise   Welcome to the group.

Elsa   Er . . . have you had to come far?

Roslyn   Not too far, no. I've got a house in Chichester.

Elsa   Oh that's nice . . .

David   Michael Parkinson lives there too.

Roslyn   Does he really? How fascinating.

Louise   We'd only just started the meeting really . . . We were just getting to know each other and taking it in turns to talk about our experiences . . .

Elsa   My daughter had just been talking about how she lost her husband . . .

Roslyn   I saw *The Marina Walker Show.* I felt so angry. It brought back so many memories. And I did so feel for you.

Elsa   And then it's on the local news that the boy's got a record deal out of it.

Roslyn   Well, I happen to know that Marina herself is not at all happy about the way the show went . . .

Elsa   And I suppose you know her personally too?

Roslyn   Yes I do . . . and she has admitted to me, off the record, of course –

Elsa   Oh, of course . . .

Roslyn   . . . that she had let things get a little out of control. She said that she is still right behind you, and she'd be willing to have you back on the show –

Louise (*interrupting*)   I wouldn't go back on there if they paid me!

Roslyn   You mean they didn't? Honestly?

Louise   We got our travel.

Roslyn   Now that is very bad. There's supposed to be an agreement on these things, but of course no one sticks to it. Unless you know you can demand payment, they'll take advantage. It's only human.

David   Esther's going to pay you one million.

Elsa   So, like David, you work in television, Rosalyn?

Roslyn   It's two syllables.

Elsa   It's what?

Roslyn   It's Ros-lyn, not Ros-a-lyn.

Elsa   I expect people are always getting it wrong.

Roslyn   Not really.

David   Did you know Richard and Judy aren't really married?

Roslyn   Is that right?

She turns to **Louise**.

Louise, I'd really like to help you build this self-help group
. . . into a charity helping many thousands of people. I'd like
to help you get your voice heard, your story told, the way
you want it told. And through that ensure your husband's
name is never forgotten . . .

David (*to* **Elsa**)   They're actually brother and sister.

Louise   I don't quite understand . . .

Roslyn   Let me tell you what happened to me. May I?

She addresses the 'group'.

Roslyn   When I was nineteen my younger sister was killed
while crossing the road. The man whose reckless driving
ended her life at fourteen was the very successful owner of a
string of nightclubs around the area. He was always being
pictured in the papers at some glitzy event or other. He had
a country house, a string of sports cars – all the trappings of
success. And of course he could afford the very best lawyers
who made sure that my sister's death didn't even cost him
his licence.

Roslyn's *voice cracks with emotion. She stands.* **Louise** *goes to her.*

Louise   That's exactly why I need to form a group to try
to fight these kinds of injustices.

David   Esther's going to help us.

Roslyn   What I'm saying is we all have it within our
powers to do something *individually*. The man who mowed
down my sister no longer lives in a big house, and I doubt if
he even owns a car, since his business empire crashed and
he was declared bankrupt. And his downfall is all due to me.

Louise *stares at* **Roslyn**, *hooked.*

Roslyn   And believe me, Louise, ruining that bastard's life
did feel good. I still miss my little sister, of course I do. But I
don't feel guilty, because I didn't sit back and let the bastard
get away with it. Now he too knows something about loss.

Louise   How did you do it? How did you ruin him?

Roslyn   With a sustained campaign in the media.

Louise   I've been trying to do that. I keep writing to the local papers . . .

Elsa   She had three letters in the *Argus* last week alone . . .

Roslyn *shakes her head.*

Roslyn   You need to think much bigger, Louise.

Louise   And you want to help me do that . . . ?

Roslyn   We could work together, side by side . . .

Louise   I don't . . . do you charge?

Roslyn   I take a small commission.

David (*to* **Roslyn**)   I could get you on Richard and Judy.

Roslyn (*to* **Louise**)   Look, perhaps we could meet, up in town, sometime later in the week . . .

She checks her Filofax.

How does Thursday sound?

Louise   I don't think I'm doing anything.

Roslyn   Terrific. If you're coming up by train to Victoria, my office is only a brief walk away. Down by the river.

Blackout.

Scene Four

A rehearsal studio.

A **Stylist** *is showing some clothes to* **Nicky** *and* **Evan**. **Phil** *is on his mobile.*

Stylist   Strong colours, lime and purples . . . softly structured jackets in fabrics like silk and satin . . .

Evan　Look at that, Nicky.

Stylist　These are from next season's collections, so you'll be ahead of the trends . . . we've Alexander McQueen, we've Dolce and Gabbana, and there's the possibility of lucrative sponsorship deals with some of these designers . . .

Phil (*on phone*)　Yeah, yeah, I understand, I'll talk to him . . . yeah, I don't see any problems, no.

Evan　This is what I'm wearing.

Stylist　Well, let's just try a few other ideas . . . look, try this.

Evan *tries a jacket, unwillingly.* **Phil** *puts the phone away.*

Phil　Nicky, a quick word . . .

Nicky　All this, it's amazing . . . you've done really well for us, Phil.

Stylist　I like that . . .

Evan　No.

He takes the jacket off.

I'm wearing my combats.

Stylist　Combats are so passé, they're *everywhere*. What we need is to create a street image which is fresh and now . . .

Phil　Nicky, look . . . I'm not sure about Evan.

Nicky　What?

Phil　I think it might be better if just you do the interview.

Nicky　No way, Phil. It's as much his band as mine. We're a team, I write the lyrics, he writes the tunes . . .

Stylist (*to* **Evan**)　Feel this, it's cashmere . . .

Evan　I'm not wearing a fucking cardy. It's bloody Steptoe, innit.

Stylist　Try it. Let's experiment.

Evan *tries the cardigan.*

Phil   All I'm saying, because it's your first serious, in-depth interview, and the way you come across is so crucial, we think it should just be the singer's opinions we focus on.

Nicky   No . . .

Stylist   It looks fantastic. Great colours.

Evan   Allied fucking Carpets.

Evan *discards the cardy in disgust.*

Phil   See, it's essential they take you seriously. That they see you as someone with a fresh angle. This is a chance for you to get your whole philosophy across . . .

Nicky   Evan can do that as well as I can. He's a pretty philosophical guy.

Evan (*to* **Stylist**)   Bollocks.

Phil   I've noticed, yeah.

His mobile phone rings.

Fuck it. (*On phone.*) Yeah . . . Great . . . yeah, next week? Yeah, fine. (*To* **Nicky** *and* **Evan**.) Guys, we're going to Morocco for the 'Hit and Run' video shoot.

Evan   Morocco? I won't need a fucking cardy in Morocco.

Nicky   Wait a minute, the video's going to be filmed in south London, in black and white. Like police camera footage.

Stylist   Black and white just isn't commercial, Nicky.

Phil   The colours of the desert will blow you away. Have you seen *The English Patient*?

Evan   You'll be a fucking patient . . . The video's got to be real – gritty.

Phil   Deserts are gritty. There'll be this big American car . . .

Stylist   A classic sixties Studebaker, driving through the sand dunes. You'll be standing on its roof playing the song . . .

Nicky   No, we're not in the video.

Phil   You have to be. You're unknowns. You've got to be U2 or REM before you can make arty, black-and-white videos without you in them. This has to be shown on kids' TV, this has to sell the record.

Nicky   It'll still end with a car crash?

Stylist   The drifting sands covering the car. A really . . . evocative image.

Phil *lights a spliff.*

Nicky   Phil, I really don't –

Phil   Guys, everyone's working in your interests here. Just sit back and enjoy the ride. Now, before this journo arrives, there's a couple of areas where you've got to tread carefully . . . Firstly, regarding drugs of all kinds – keep 'em guessing.

He passes the spliff to **Nicky**.

Drugs are cool, but I don't want to read in the tabloids that someone's sixteen-year-old daughter's in a coma or a coffin after following the example of her heroes Alice Don't Surf.

Nicky   We'll be careful. I don't want to get done for anything else.

The **Stylist** *brings* **Evan** *some more clothes.*

Stylist   One or two of these may be more you.

Phil   Remember the America thing too. Even talking about drugs might be enough to fuck the bands transatlantic prospects. Another big thing – don't mention girlfriends. We want to gain as big a female audience as possible . . . and research shows that girl fans like to fantasise about being in with a chance . . . But it's still a good idea to mention something about girls – tell him you've already built a loyal female following, blah blah blah.

Evan   Yeah, that's why we decided to start a band. To meet girls.

Nicky   Evan wants to be a chick-magnet.

Evan *tries a tight, shiny jacket.*

Phil   You will, believe me. But in the meantime you mustn't give the impression you live like monks, or that there's any possibility you might be gay. Gay's cool for dance acts, but it's not a good selling point for guitar-based rock.

Evan   We're one hundred per cent not gay. I was in the paras, did he tell you?

Phil   Here he is . . . the journo.

Evan   He looks like a tosser.

Nicky   Look, why don't I talk to him, while you're picking out your gear . . .

Evan   That's Phil's idea, right? Keep me out of the fucking interviews . . .

Enter **Greg** *carrying a tape recorder. He clocks the tension.*

Nicky   No, Evan . . .

Evan   Just as you'll let him stick 'Hit and Run' in the fucking Sahara.

Greg   Hi, guys, like, I'm sorry I'm late.

Evan *turns away.* **Greg** *sits down with* **Nicky**. **Phil** *goes to the back to make a call.*

Greg   Well, Nicky, your band gained itself a manager, a string of gigs and a record deal, all on the back of an appearance on *The Marina Walker Show* . . . so how are you coping with virtually overnight success?

Nicky   Things are good, yeah.

Evan   Where's my bullet belt?

Greg   Now 'Hit and Run' has crashed into this week's singles chart at number twenty-six –

Nicky   *Crashed* into the chart – That's a song dealing with a serious experience – that's three minutes forty-one seconds of what it's like to kill somebody.

Greg   I've touched a raw nerve?

Nicky   It's not something to be treated lightly, that's all. I'm not saying all our songs are going to be about . . . heavy emotional shit . . .

Evan   Darkness and death . . .

Nicky   . . . but, well, that one is about something I have to live with.

Greg   And the message of the song is drive carefully?

Nicky   It's not like it's trying to be the musical equivalent of some public information film . . .

Evan   Like the one James Dean made before he crashed.

Stylist   Evan, let's think footwear . . .

Nicky   No, it kinda leaves things open. Leaves you to make your own decision.

Greg   On what? To speed or not to speed?

Nicky   No, on a deeper level, it makes you think about things like fate and destiny.

Greg   Like, was it Darren Fielder's destiny to be killed by you in a road accident?

Nicky   That kind of question, yeah.

Greg   And was Darren merely put on this earth to become the catalyst that made Alice Don't Surf a hit band?

Nicky   No, that's bollocks. That's shit.

Greg   This hostile front, Nicky, is it a pose on behalf of the band's image, or is it some kind of self-protection?

Nicky   I don't know what you're getting at.

Greg   I think what I'm asking is how deeply do you think killing a man, albeit accidentally, has affected you?

Phil *joins* **Nicky**.

Nicky   I'm trying to put that completely behind me.

Greg   But if you wanted to forget it, would you have written a song about it?

Nicky   I wrote the song to help me deal with it.

Greg   Because you went public, on television, and talked about what happened, do you think that's going to make it harder for people to forget about it? I mean, people are always going to ask you about it, aren't they?

Phil   No, all that'll be forgotten in six months' time.

Greg   But the band won't be, Nicky?

Nicky   We're here for keeps.

Greg   How do you want people to feel towards Alice Don't Surf? Do you want people to like you?

Nicky   I don't care. If people are too stupid to see how good we are, it's their problem.

Greg   Do you want people to hate you? Say, this is me, I killed someone and if you can't handle that it's your problem – shove it all in their faces?

Nicky   I don't think I'm that negative.

Greg   And what about love?

Evan   We don't do love songs.

Nicky   It's all been said before.

Greg What about the love from your fans – at the Mean Fiddler the other night the mostly teenage audience seemed to be identifying with your lyrics about rejection and pain.

Nicky The girls I've talked to after our gigs weren't asking about the meaning of life . . . they just wanted to fuck something famous or almost famous.

Greg You refer to yourself as something, not someone?

Nicky I was talking about the band.

Greg Are you party animals . . . into the whole sex and drugs thing . . .?

Phil There's a lot of paranoia about the drugs thing, Greg . . .

Nicky From Phil mainly.

Greg But you do use?

Nicky No.

Greg Never? Nothing at all? Even talking off the record?

Nicky We don't believe in 'off the record'.

Greg Alice Don't Surf has an anti-drugs stance then?

Nicky Oh . . . er, definitely, yeah. You've got to be clean to make good music . . .

Greg So what would you say about Oasis and East 17 . . .

Nicky Case proven.

Greg Have you or Evan got a girlfriend at the moment?

Evan Even *Smash Hits* didn't ask that.

Greg But you say you're getting a fair bit of attention from the opposite sex. How does that feel?

Nicky I can handle it.

Evan Except when they send you shit-a-grams, and break your windows.

Greg   Fuck, has that kind of thing been happening? Are you saying you're the victim of a hate campaign?

Phil   Er, look, we're going to have to cut things short now, guys, we've a radio session to record . . .

Blackout.

Scene Five

The seating area. Glossy magazines and coffees on the table.

Enter **Roslyn** *and* **Louise**.

Louise (*hushed*)   I need the loo.

Roslyn   Again?

Louise   Won't be a minute.

Exit **Louise**.

Enter **Justine**, *a features editor.* **Justine** *and* **Roslyn** *hug and kiss.*

Justine   I do appreciate this, Roslyn. I know Kate's your *friend*.

Roslyn   She understands how it is.

Justine   She still must be absolutely gutted to lose this one, especially to us of all people.

Roslyn   It seems very short-sighted of them, but maybe they really couldn't go any higher.

Justine   You'd think they'd be prepared to put a little more on table . . . still, their loss is our gain . . .

Roslyn   And you are still interested in the serialisation rights?

Justine   Very. If she does write the book . . .

Roslyn   She will.

Justine   And I can just see the movie . . .

Roslyn   So can we.

Enter **Louise**.

Roslyn   Louise, meet Justine, a very old friend of mine. Louise has been getting a little bit nervous . . .

Justine   Do sit down. That's your coffee there. Well, there's nothing at all to be nervous about . . .

Louise   My dentist always says that.

Justine   Mine too, isn't that extraordinary? But this is going to be nothing like a trip to the dentist, I can assure you. Now, Louise, you're up for the day from where exactly?

Louise   Littlehampton.

Justine   And where *exactly* is –

Roslyn   It's the south coast. A stone's throw from my new place at Chichester.

Justine   Oh yeah, how are you liking living in the country, Ros? It must take quite a while to adapt to all that quiet. Miles of trees and . . . quiet. Is Littlehampton a village, Louise?

Louise   No, it's a town.

Roslyn   Louise lives on the river.

Justine   In a boat?

Louise   A . . . chalet backing on to the river.

Justine   A chalet.

Louise   It's kind of like a large caravan that used to be part of a holiday camp, but it isn't any more . . .

Justine   Got ya. Like an American trailer park? Is it rough? I mean, is there a criminal problem? Drugs and so forth?

Louise   It's mainly old people.

Justine   And it's run-down?

Louise   A bit, yeah.

Justine   You live there with your husband?

Roslyn   Justine, Louise's husband was killed.

Justine   Oh, I'm so, so sorry. What a stupid, *stupid* . . . I'm just having a really hectic day. I'm sorry, Louise, do forgive me.

Louise   It's OK . . .

Justine   No, it was unforgivable. And so insensitive. Can you tell us a little bit more about yourself? What do you do?

Louise   I make sandwiches. And sell them to local convenience stores.

Justine   How interesting. So you've got like a little sandwich empire down there in wossit-on-sea.

Louise   Littlehampton.

Justine   And do you make lots of money? Our readers are always interested in hearing of women who have their own businesses, especially those who work from home . . .

Louise   I don't make anything hardly at all . . . it's just to give me a bit on top of my dole to try and pay off some debts. Shit, you probably didn't ought to mention about the sandwich thing. I probably didn't still ought to be claiming the Job Seekers Allowance . . .

Justine   You have financial difficulties. I understand.

Louise   I used to run a business with my husband. We'd just opened this little DIY shop in Bognor when he was killed . . .

Justine (*murmurs*)   So tragic.

Louise   Course we still owed on all the stock and we
hadn't finished sorting out the shop lease with the bank. So
everything collapsed leaving me with these huge debts. I've
had to let our flat go and move back in with my mum.

Justine   On the river? So you've got a nice view at least. I
always think that's the worst thing about living in London.
You have to be incredibly lucky to live somewhere with a
view . . . So, Louise, you were invited on to *The Marina
Walker Show* to talk about your tragic loss . . .

Roslyn   Louise felt the show, albeit unintentionally,
trivialised her situation . . .

Justine   While launching Nicky Farrell's band into the big
time.

Roslyn *smiles.*

Justine   Say, did you hear about that shooting that
happened after an American talk show?

Louise   Yes, and I can understand that.

Justine   If you had a gun and Nicky Farrell in your
sights . . .

Louise   I don't know . . . He should've been locked up.
He killed my husband –

Justine   An eye for an eye, oh absolutely.

Louise   I'm talking to you as part of my campaign to get
justice for people like Darren.

Roslyn   Louise is a very strong, determined woman. That
was the first thing that struck me when we met. She is going
to get her revenge, make no doubt about it.

Justine   And we're all one hundred per cent behind you,
Louise. You won't believe the compassion and warmth of
our readers.

Louise   Are you going to mention him in the article?

Justine   Darren? Of course.

Louise   Farrell. It'll be more publicity for him, won't it?

Roslyn   Remember what I explained to you on the train up? There's good publicity and there's bad publicity . . .

Justine   You're getting the good publicity, and he'll get the bad.

Louise   All publicity is good publicity.

Roslyn   It doesn't work like that.

Justine   Absolutely not. Roslyn was telling me you think Farrell was under the influence of drugs when he ran down your husband.

Louise   I said I thought it was possible.

Enter a photographer, **Guido***, with camera and tripod.*

Justine   That is such an important issue, Louise. Drink-driving gets all the publicity, but junkies are getting away with driving dangerously and putting lives at risk. I think that'll make a very strong introduction to our piece.

Guido *coughs.*

Justine   Oh, hi, Guido. Oh, are you waiting for us?

She gets up.

I'll leave you all to it then.

Guido *moves the chair in front of the camera and ushers* **Louise** *back into it.*

Exit **Justine***.*

Guido   Justine's just great, isn't she? And she'll write a piece you can be proud of. She's a way of expressing people's thoughts for them better than they could themselves . . . People she's interviewed always say that. Often, they're really moved when they read what she's written. Need a little bit more light here . . . that's more like it.

I used to do mainly fashion shoots. Travel the world – spring pastel cardies in the Alps, spicy sarongs in Jamaica, but I much prefer being on features because you get to meet so many incredible *real* people. You see terminal cancers, babies born without arms, women in abusive relationships . . . and when you see the human spirit struggling through so much adversity, it's humbling. And I know it's a massive cliché but it does make you count your blessings.

He moves behind **Louise** *with a light meter.*

Littlehampton's lovely. Took my wind-surfing rig down there with me. Beautiful day, but plenty of wind. I'm so envious of you, Louise, having a river in your backyard.

Louise   So why were you in Littlehampton?

Guido   Getting a few background photos.

Roslyn   This is going to be *your* story, Louise. The readers will want to know all about what it's like to be you – what your home looks like . . . what it's like to live there. It's all to help them identify and empathise.

Guido   I was very moved seeing your husband's grave.

Louise   Were the flowers dead? I meant to put some fresh flowers on it this week. I usually do . . .

Guido   I had some fresh flowers with me. I hope you don't mind, but I left them there.

Louise   I feel terrible. I really meant to change the flowers.

Guido   That's right, relax.

The shutter whirrs.

Good. Did you remember to bring your photo?

Louise *takes a framed photo of a man from her handbag.* **Guido** *adjust her position. He looks through the viewfinder, moves her slightly.*

Guido   There. That's it. Hold it like that. Let all the memories come flooding back.

Roslyn   Remember everything Darren meant to you. All the laughter you shared.

Guido   Lift your head a little. That's it.

Louise   I'm sorry, baby. I'm sorry about the flowers.

Guido   Nice. Very nice. One more. Fantastic, Louise. Right, that's it.

Roslyn   You're a pro, Louise.

Guido *moves closer to* **Louise**.

Guido   Is that a tear? It is.

He moves closer.

Tell me to piss off if you think I'm getting too intrusive, yeah?

Louise   You'll get my spots and wrinkles.

Roslyn   Trust me, Louise, it's looking good.

Guido *wipes his eyes.*

Guido   You've got me at it now. Only need to see someone else crying and off I go.

Roslyn   Guido, are you about ready to wrap up here. We've got to be at *Women Today* by three.

Exit **Guido**.

Louise *and* **Roslyn** *get up.*

Roslyn   I thought your interview went very well, don't you?

Louise   She didn't ask anything about Darren or the self-help group.

Roslyn   I'd already briefed her on all the details. She just needed to meet you. Everything'll be in the article. Justine's known for her crusading journalism. That's why I picked her.

Louise   She didn't know Darren's dead.

Roslyn   She did. She was a little bit pissed, that's all . . .

Louise   I wish I hadn't said about my debts. It'll look like I'm doing this for the money.

Roslyn   We have full editorial control. Nothing goes into print without your approval. Anything you and I don't like – out it goes.

Louise   Thanks, Roslyn.

Blackout.

Scene Six

A hotel bar. **Roslyn** *is chatting with a Waiter.*

Enter **Nicky**. *The Waiter drifts away.* **Nicky** *comes up behind* **Roslyn***, grabs her from behind, surprising her.*

Nicky   'Hit and Run' drops out of the Top Ten, our album's stuck at twenty-four, and now I've been driven out of my home – all due to you and your professional fucking widow!

Roslyn *breaks free of* **Nicky**'s *grasp and turns to face him.*

Roslyn   What . . . ? Now just you listen –

Nicky *snatches hold of her wrists.*

Nicky   No, *you* listen. I've had about all I can take. You're making my life hell. All the papers fucking write about is the hate campaign against me. I've had people shouting and jeering outside my house day and night . . . I've had to leave my home . . . I drove back down to see my mum and some bastards trashed my new car . . .

Roslyn   You can't lay all your problems at my door,
Nicky . . .

Pause. She smiles into his face.

And a degree of notoriety is sometimes no bad thing . . .

Nicky   I want to be known for my music, not for
squashing Darren Fielder.

Roslyn   Naturally, but it is what helps keep your name in
the papers. There're hundreds of chart bands, but only
yours has a singer who ran down a pedestrian. So you
pancaked Fielder. If you hadn't, the next car probably
would've. For all you know he could've had terminal
cancer, he could've been suicidal. We've all got to die
sometime . . .

Nicky *breaks away from* **Roslyn**.

Nicky   You can't say I did the guy a favour.

Roslyn   I'm saying you don't need to spend your whole
life at confession.

Nicky *sits down.*

Nicky   Well, you invited me here. You asked for this
meeting, Roslyn. So what can you do for me?

Roslyn   I can stop this hate campaign.

Nicky   How?

Roslyn   By changing the way you're presented in the
media. By showing you as a young man with hidden depths,
a tortured soul. Someone who's been to hell and back, an
got to know himself along the way, someone who *cares*. Now
you mentioned visiting your mum. That's one positive,
caring image you've already given me.

Nicky   I don't know about bringing my mum into this. It's
been really rough on her, reading shit like how I was stoned
when I killed Fielder, and how I was laughing in court. It's
all fucking lies.

Roslyn   How do your record company feel about the idea of you having a personal publicist?

Nicky   They're as worried as I am about the negative stories. But what about Louise Fielder? How can you represent both of us?

Roslyn   I can make sure any further publicity I generate for Louise doesn't work against you. You must stop seeing her as the enemy. She's more of a team-mate really. And look at what I've done for her. You can't tell me you're not impressed. That's the reason you've agreed to meet me, isn't it?

Nicky   And you're here because you sense the chance of making *big* money. If you can achieve so much with a nobody, think where you could take me.

Roslyn   Providing you had the right kind of attitude . . . and I thought I could work with you. Now, Louise doesn't have immediate media appeal, I grant you, but she's willing to learn . . .

Nicky   Whereas my band's outstanding.

Roslyn   You have a wider talent base to build on, admitted.

Nicky   So why aren't we on the magazine covers? Why isn't it us with the big interviews and pictures? People missed our radio sessions because they weren't heralded by a big blast of publicity.

Roslyn   You're not big because you don't think big. I've read your interviews in the music press. They're fine in their way but there is the 'so what?' factor. I didn't come away wanting to hear the record, steal the poster or buy the shirt.

Nicky   You don't think we had anything new or original to say?

Roslyn   No one has anything new and original to say, believe me.

Nicky   So? What do you actually think I should do?

Roslyn   Are you seriously interested in working with me, or just in picking my brains?

Nicky   Fax our manager your contract.

Roslyn *smiles.*

Roslyn   Very well. Now, you've been espousing very safe opinions – say no to drugs, respect for women . . . My daddy wouldn't disagree with any of that. Or my granny.

Nicky   So what would you suggest? Smoke a joint at an after-show party, screw somebody else's girl?

Roslyn   For the moment just be aware of opportunities. Look for a chance we could turn into a headline.

Waiter comes in with drinks on a tray. **Roslyn** *takes one for herself and one for* **Nicky**.

Nicky   Have you told Louise we're going to be working together?

Roslyn   Not yet.

Nicky   I'd love to see her face.

Blackout.

Act Two

Scene One

Backstage at the Astoria. The radio is on.

Nicky *and* **Evan** *are getting ready for the gig.* **Evan** *has a pile of clothes which he's trying on. He offers* **Nicky** *a particularly nasty cardigan.*

Evan   You might want this if you're gonna be on a magazine.

Nicky   I don't think I'm going to wearing that much in the photo.

Evan   What? You're going to be naked? On a magazine? That's disgusting.

Nicky   Thanks.

Evan   That's pornography.

Nicky   Don't be stupid. It'll be tasteful. Just my top half or something.

Evan   And it'll just be you in the picture? Not me, not the rest of the guys?

Nicky   It's the *Face*, Evan, not the Faces.

Evan   Yeah, well, it's not just your *face* they want, is it? I don't see why they can't have less of you, and find some room in the photo for the rest of us. It's all that Roslyn's idea, isn't it? Keep all the glory for you and her. What is it, do you two have some kind of thing going on? You like older women all of a sudden, is that it?

Nicky   You look a prat in that shirt.

Evan   You're sure you want me right at the front of the stage beside you? You're sure you don't want me to keep out of sight, eh? Or maybe you don't need me at all any more. Perhaps you want to play this fucking guitar!

Nicky   Evan . . .

Enter **Phil**.

Phil   Nicky, Evan, guess who I've brought to see you?

Enter **Marina**, *a little overdressed.*

Marina   Hi, guys. (*To* **Evan**.) Nice shirt.

Nicky   Marina . . . hi . . . er, sit down . . . can I get you something to drink? A beer?

Marina   Thanks.

Nicky *rushes to get her a beer.* **Evan** *puts his combat jacket on.*

Marina   I've been following your progress with great interest.

Nicky   Yeah, well, if it wasn't for your show . . .

Marina   Exactly, a star is born thanks to Marina Walker.

Phil *gets out the cocaine.*

Phil   Here we go, guys.

He cuts it.

Nicky   Ladies first.

Marina *snorts the coke.*

Evan   The set list . . . where's the set list?

Nicky   It's here.

Marina   Are you nervous, Evan?

Marina *offers* **Evan** *a line of coke.*

Phil   Er, not too much . . .

Nicky *takes* **Phil** *to one side.*

Nicky   Have you seen about sacking the driver?

Phil   Not yet, Nicky . . .

Nicky   For fuck's sake . . .

Evan   It's good shit, eh, Marina?

Phil   I mean, don't you think you might be overreacting? I haven't noticed him doing anything dangerous.

Evan (*to* **Marina**)   You're looking really nice . . .

Nicky   He's a fucking madman. His driving's lethal . . .

Marina *gets up.* **Phil** *notices.*

Phil   Look, we'll discuss this later, right?

Nicky   I keep telling him when he needs to slow down . . . and he just fucking ignores it. Every time that guy puts his foot down, I'm getting flashbacks . . .

Evan   And all you do is go on about the bloke's driving – it's really starting to piss me off.

Marina *is leaving.*

Phil   Look, we'll talk later, right guys. Have a good one.

Exit **Phil**, *after* **Marina**.

On the radio, the DJ cuts in.

DJ   Our first guest on this evening's discussion and phone-in is Louise Fielder/

Nicky   Oh fuck.

Louise *and a female* **DJ** *enter the seated area. Both are wearing headphones. The* **DJ** *sets up a microphone between them.*

DJ   Welcome to the programme, Louise.

Louise   It's good to be here, Penny.

Evan *moves to switch the radio off.*

Nicky   No, turn it up. Better see what she's on about this time.

Evan   Forewarned is forearmed, yeah?

DJ   As usual our lines will be open all evening, and your call should cost no more than 40p a minute, no matter where you're calling from.

Evan   Fucking rip-off.

DJ   If you're not the bill-payer in your household, make sure that person knows you're calling. Now, tonight's discussion is on that evil plaguing so many people's lives –

Nicky   Her!

DJ   . . . drug abuse.

Nicky   And oh don't tell me – Louise is the world expert all of a sudden.

Nicky *and* **Evan** *talk over the* **DJ** *and* **Louise***'s lines.*

DJ   So call now, if you want to voice your concerns on tonight's phone-in topic – drug abuse. Our operators are waiting to take your calls.

Evan   Like she was the expert on the banning of 'Crash' last week.

Nicky   Bet she's never even seen it . . .

DJ   Now, Louise, a recent newspaper survey showed that fifty-nine per cent of sixteen-year-olds had experimented with drugs. Did that figure shock or surprise you?

Nicky *takes out his mobile phone.*

Louise   It didn't surprise me, Penny, but it did make me feel very sad. I don't remember there being anything like that kind of problem with drugs when I was at school . . .

Evan   What're you doing?

DJ   And do you think that the figures are right? I mean, some kids might've been exaggerating just to impress the researchers, mightn't they?

Nicky   Fuck, it's engaged.

Louise   Just the fact that they feel they need to boast about something like that is very sad indeed . . .

Evan   We're on stage in five minutes.

Nicky *dials again.*

DJ   Would you say a big part of the problem is peer pressure then? – Kids wanting to do the trendy thing and keep in with their mates?

Nicky   Oh, hi, I'd like to take part in your phone-in.

Evan   Nicky!

Nicky   Yeah, I'll hold.

Louise   But I think the media is also in some ways responsible for the current crisis. I mean, so many movies and pop groups now seem to be glamorising drug abuse . . .

Evan   Come on, man. You ain't got time to fuck about.

DJ   It's easy to say the media is guilty of this, or guilty of that. But if that's really the case, aren't we all equally guilty for buying into their vision? I mean, we all go to see those movies, don't we? We all buy those groups' CDs.

Louise   I wouldn't say we *all* do, Penny . . .

DJ   Many of us, then. Time to go to the phones. Caller on line three. You're through to the studio.

Nicky   Can I ask Louise a question?

DJ   What's your name, caller, and where are you calling from?

Nicky   Nicky Farrell, formerly from Littlehampton . . . er, currently backstage at the Astoria.

Evan   And supposed to be on fucking stage.

DJ   Well . . . Nicky . . . what a surprise and wonderful to know you listen to the programme. This certainly is the station the stars listen to . . .

Nicky *makes a face at* **Evan** *who ignores him.*

DJ   So you're playing a gig tonight to promote your new album, which incidentally we've been playing here all week and was record of the week last week on the breakfast show . . .

Nicky   Can I talk to Louise?

DJ   Yeah, sure. Do you want to give your gig a bit of a plug first – and get our listeners rushing down there . . .

Nicky   It's already sold out, unfortunately . . .

DJ   Oh, that's fantastic –

Nicky   Is Louise still there?

DJ (*slightly uncertain*)   Louise, do you want to talk to Nicky?

Louise   I don't think he should be doing this . . . harassing me like this. My lawyers said they'd get a writ.

Nicky   You mean an injunction. I think you'll find that's what you need. That's what I'm getting to block the publication of your book.

DJ   You're writing a book, Louise?

Nicky   She's wasting her time if she is.

DJ   OK now, this is supposed to be a discussion about the damage done to people's lives by drugs.

Nicky   That's what I rang in about. I wanted to make the point that there are other things out there which are damaging people's lives, and not getting the same amount of publicity.

DJ   Such as?

Nicky   Such as Louise's personal vendetta against me. I've had to leave my home in Littlehampton, after having slogans daubed on the walls, my windows broken and shit through the letter box. My new car's had paint stripper thrown over it and the wheels pinched . . .

DJ Sounds like you parked it in the wrong area, eh?

Evan Come on, come on.

Louise That had nothing to do with me.

Nicky It has everything to do with you. You go on radio and TV just to incite that kind of hatred against me –

Louise That's ridiculous. I do nothing of the sort. You're paranoid –

Nicky Yeah, sure – I can't even go into a pub on my own any more. Fortunately our guitarist is an ex-para or I'd have to start thinking about getting a bodyguard.

DJ This is supposed to be a discussion about drugs, Nicky.

Nicky I was coming to that. That's the whole reason I rang in. I want to ask Louise exactly what she knows about drugs. How come she's setting herself up as an expert on the subject?

DJ Louise?

Louise I'm not an expert. I'm a concerned ordinary person.

Nicky Come on, you're coming on the radio to offer your prejudiced opinions on something you know nothing about.

DJ You're listening to Chat Radio, your twenty-four-hour quality chat and pop station. Our lines are open now if you want to talk to Louise Fielder and Nicky Farrell. Remember, premium rates apply. Ask the bill-payer before you call.

Louise I know drugs are dangerous . . .

Nicky Not good enough. Which drugs? Facts? Statistics?

Louise You want facts? Fact one. You'd have to be very stupid to take any kind of illegal substance.

Nicky Many thousands of people listening in right now know you're talking arse. They use speed, ecstasy or whatever on a regular basis, every week, year in, year out,

with no ill effects . . . But they're not going to get the chance
to express their views, and challenge the blinkered,
uninformed opinions of the likes of you.

DJ   And do you use drugs, Nicky?

Nicky   I have done . . . I mean, I go through phases . . . I
must've tried just about everything in the last three months .
. . since my car accident . . . from amps and ecstasy to
cocaine . . . as a kind of therapy, I suppose . . . I mean, if I'd
gone to the doctor he'd have only sent me away with some
drug or other.

Louise   Were you taking drugs when you killed my
Darren?

Nicky   No. But now I have to get off my face before I can
even think about getting behind the wheel . . .

Evan   We're on stage, man!

He snatches the phone.

Forget her, Nicky. Come on.

Blackout.

Scene Two

The television news programme begins in the blackout.

Elsa *piles packs of sandwiches into a basket while watching telly.*

Newsreader   . . . that report from George Masters,
outside Parliament. And now back to tonight's main story/

Elsa *points the remote at the video to 'record'.*

Newsreader   /The pro-drugs outburst on Chat Radio by
Alice Don't Surf's singer Nicky Farrell. Earlier this evening,
live on air, Farrell admitted that he drives while under the
influence of ecstasy, amphetamines and cocaine. The
singer's admission has already led to widespread

condemnation, with several radio stations dropping the group's record from their playlists, while a number of high street stores are considering removing it from their shelves. Earlier this year, Farrell was convicted of dangerous driving, when he failed to stop after killing a pedestrian. Seen an hour ago, entering a West End club with a mystery woman, Nicky Farrell declined the opportunity to comment on the furore or offer any kind of apology.

And tonight's other news again in brief . . . Today at the Treasury . . .

Elsa *switches off the TV, hearing* **Louise** *coming in.*

Enter **Louise**. *She slumps on the sofa.*

Louise   I'm shattered.

Elsa   I thought you said you'd be back by eight.

Louise   Yeah, it's been mad – had reporters calling me at Chat Radio before we'd even gone off-air.

Elsa   You don't think you're over doing it? You look really tired.

Louise   I am tired. But I've got to take this opportunity while I'm hot news.

Elsa   You'd better leave delivering this lot 'til the morning, I suppose.

Louise   I've got to be in London by nine.

Elsa   Someone's got to deliver them, after I spent all day making them.

Louise   Well, you didn't need to.

Pause.

I told you I'm getting paid for talking to the papers now. We don't need to make sandwiches any more.

Elsa   You've still got to deliver these. The shops will be expecting them.

Louise It doesn't matter, OK?

Louise *gets up, pulls a magazine away from under* **Elsa***'s work area, brushes the crumbs off it.*

Elsa Letting people down doesn't matter. (*Pause.*) You've really changed, Louise . . . since you began this whole thing with Roslyn . . .

Louise Course I've changed. I've had to change . . . Now that I don't have Darren to be strong for me.

Elsa I don't remember Darren being strong. It was always you sorting out his problems . . .

Louise Mum . . .

Elsa Well, it's true, isn't it? The hours you put in, in that shop – which was supposed to be your joint business. And where was Darren? More often than not, down the pub with his mates.

Louise That's where he had to take people . . . for business. The DIY shop would've been a success if it had had a chance to get going. That's why it's so important for me to find something else to do with my life . . . to give me a purpose.

Elsa What about your self-help group? That was going to be your 'purpose', wasn't it? When are you going to get that off the ground?

Louise As soon as I've time. I've loads of letters from people interested in joining . . . and that's because they've read about it in the magazines or heard me on the radio. Roslyn says it's crucial to get the right level of publicity first.

Elsa So have you been able to write back to any of these people?

Louise Not yet.

Elsa Because you're never here long enough, are you? You go rushing off to London every day and I end up doing

all your washing, and getting your meals which are always
ruined because you're never in on time.

Louise   Alright . . . you don't need to cook for me. I'll eat
some of these bloody sandwiches. Yeah, look, I know things
have been a bit crazy these last few weeks . . . but you told
me you didn't mind . . . you've been as excited as I have,
reading the articles . . . and showing them to your friends.

Elsa   The only way I get to know what my daughter's
thinking or feeling is reading it in a magazine.

Louise   Don't be stupid, Mum . . . and a lot of that stuff
isn't what I actually said anyway. But Roslyn makes sure
they don't say anything bad about me, and now tomorrow's
papers will bring the drug-driving message into millions of
homes.

Elsa   And you'll be recognised everywhere you go . . .
more people staring and pointing at you in the street . . .

Louise   I know, but getting a higher profile is the only
way I'm going to get a proper job . . . as a radio or TV
presenter.

Elsa   Roslyn was going to have a word with Chat Radio
about giving you a job, wasn't she?

Louise   The thing is, they're not that interested, not yet
. . . because I'm not a big enough name . . . but they've
invited me on as a guest again next week . . .

Elsa   Well, I hope they put you in a hotel this time. I don't
like you having to travel home so late . . .

Louise   I'll get her to ask them. She's really great like that
. . . and she always stops the interview if I'm getting too
tired, or upset or anything.

Elsa   Louise . . . I think you should see this, love.

Elsa *goes to switch on the TV.*

Blackout.

Scene Three

Roslyn *sits on a bench by the river, with a takeaway, wearing a party dress and sunglasses.*

Enter **Nicky**, *also in shades.*

Roslyn   At last . . .

Nicky   Yeah, well . . . my flat got firebombed.

Roslyn   Oh my God.

Nicky   I went straight home to bed after I'd left you . . . must've been five-ish. Woke up about eight and, like, the room was full of smoke. The police reckon someone had pushed burning newspapers in the window.

Roslyn   Are you all right? You're not hurt?

Nicky   No thanks to your Louise. All the furniture, most of my clothes and two guitars – totally fucked. Louise'll have a great big fucking grin on her face when she reads about this. Yeah, why don't you call her? Get your phone out and ring her.

Roslyn   It'll be on the news . . . even in Littlehampton. So do the police have any idea who might be responsible?

Nicky   They're still there rummaging about among my charred possessions. I hope cocaine's combustible. I wouldn't have reported the fire if it had been up to me. Course the old bag next door saw the smoke pouring out of my windows as a chance to get herself on TV. Now there're reporters camped outside, film crews and everything . . .

Roslyn   Yes, there were quite a few reporters outside my office this morning.

Nicky   I had to come here on the bus. I mean, I rang Phil . . . but he's not answering. I rang the record company to ask them to send a car, and couldn't get anyone to talk to me . . .

Roslyn   They may well be distancing themselves from you, because of your outburst . . .

Nicky   Christ, Roslyn, what do I do? . . . you said you'd stop her doing any more damage to my reputation.

Roslyn   This mess is hardly Louise's fault.

Nicky   No, it's *your* fault. You told me to cause a scandal.

Roslyn   Did I tell you to phone in that show and shoot your mouth off?

Nicky   Not exactly, but –

Roslyn   As I recall, I said we needed to wait for the *right* situation to arise. And that was not the right situation, Nicky. OK, the damage is done . . .

Nicky   It's a fucking disaster . . . no one will play or sell our records now . . .

Roslyn   Only for a day or so, believe me. Ultimately this slight crisis will give the band a higher media profile . . . that will pay off in terms of greater record sales – once we've reversed the bans. Now, already this morning I've managed to get the band a slot at a gig for a children's charity.

Nicky   Just don't let me get photographed with a little kid sitting on my knee . . .

Roslyn   And I've an interview lined up with an ecology magazine. The concept is it'll show Alice Don't Surf as a band with environmental concerns.

Nicky   We become dolphin huggers – all right, fine.

Roslyn   If you're only seen as shallow, hedonistic rockers the drugs stuff is more harming. If you can be seen as cerebral, cultish, a *thinking* band, people are more likely to accept what you said as opening up a sensible discussion of the issues . . . which is the line I'm currently giving the media. Most importantly of all though, you need to offer a public apology –

Nicky   No fucking way.

Roslyn   Nicky . . .

Nicky   When I apologised to Louise – said I was sorry for killing her old man, she threw it all back in my face. Well, now I'm not remotely sorry. If I hadn't splattered Fielder I'd still be on the dole. If I had the same opportunity again, I'd drive straight at the bastard.

Roslyn   Nicky, please . . . this situation doesn't just affect you –

Nicky   I've fucked things up for Evan and the guys, I know. But I don't want her in every magazine and phone-in gloating about me being made to apologise.

Roslyn   All reinforcing the view that you've changed, and you're *truly* sorry. Then whatever she says, she'll be doing half the work to get the record ban lifted for you.

Nicky   Apologising will get 'Hit and Run' straight back on the radio?

Roslyn   It might. But there is one way to virtually guarantee it. And to give your album a good chance of topping the charts. I've already spoken to Marina, and she'd be delighted to have the band back on her show, playing up to three live numbers . . .

Nicky   That's great . . . but when?

Roslyn   Tomorrow. They're willing to alter the show schedule to accommodate you, putting off to a later programme the act who would have been providing the music.

Nicky   Well done, Roz.

Roslyn   So now all I need you to do, is to keep away from the media for the next twenty-four hours.

Nicky   I'll try.

Roslyn   I know you will, and you'll come out of this stronger, wiser and even more successful. You're a survivor. You take the knocks and you bounce right back. It must take an immense amount of courage to get back behind the wheel after a bad accident, but you did. That's strength, Nicky.

Nicky   At first I swore I'd never drive again . . . but you just can't let stuff like that get to you.

Roslyn   Absolutely not. If you don't mind me asking, and tell me if you do . . . why didn't you stop at the accident?

Nicky   I don't know. I didn't think about it. I just put my foot back down. I don't remember making the decision. It just happened.

Roslyn   But you waited for a moment, to see someone was taking care of him . . .

Nicky   No . . . I only said that on the telly.

Roslyn   It wasn't true?

Nicky   No. And I didn't lie in court. I just said it on the programme to try and make her feel better.

Roslyn   I understand.

Nicky   Afterwards I felt bad about lying.

Roslyn   Sometimes we all have to lie.

Nicky   For you isn't it occupational?

Roslyn   Yes, but I think very seriously about it every time. Lying isn't something I do lightly.

Nicky   But you must be always making up stuff to gain the media's interest.

Roslyn   Building someone an image and keeping them in the headlines isn't the same as lying. It's more like storytelling, it's creating a kind of modern mythology. It's about creating heroes . . .

Nicky   And villains? So has anyone ever made up a story about you?

Roslyn   Not to my knowledge.

Nicky   Have you been on TV or the radio, yourself?

Roslyn   Now and again, to support a client.

Nicky   Would you like to be famous, in your own right?

Roslyn   Depends what you mean by famous. If I could sing or act or whatever . . .

Nicky   When you were a kid, what did you want to be?

Roslyn *laughs.*

Roslyn   I can't remember. Why do you want to know about me, anyway?

Nicky   To find out what makes you tick . . . Are you married?

Roslyn   I've been married. Just the once. I've a son – lives with his father. It's all quite amicable.

Nicky   You don't get lonely?

Roslyn   On the whole I tend to find people disappointing. They bore me.

Nicky   Do I bore you?

Roslyn   Would I be sitting on the embankment sharing a soggy takeaway if I found you boring?

Nicky   So how much trouble would I need to be in before you turned your back on me?

Roslyn   I've never been one to run from trouble.

Nicky   You think maybe you might be drawn to it?

Roslyn   Perhaps . . . now and again . . . So, what are you going to do now? You can hardly go back to a burnt-out flat . . .

Nicky   Could you find me a hotel? Just for a night or two.

Roslyn   I could, but the press might well find it too. Tell you what, you could stop over at mine. I've got a little flat in Kensington where I live during the week. You'd be welcome to stay there tonight . . . on the sofa or whatever.

Nicky   Yeah, whatever . . .

Blackout.

Scene Four

Roslyn's *office.* **Louise** *is standing around.*

Enter **Roslyn**.

Roslyn   Sorry, I was delayed. I've rung the Oxo Tower, told them we'd be a little late.

Louise   I'm not hungry. I don't want to talk. I just came here to tell you you're sacked and that's it.

Roslyn   I understand your anger, Louise . . .

Louise   I don't want you to understand. I want you to explain. What were you doing with *him*?

Roslyn   You have to trust me . . .

Louise   I did. Before I saw you on the news with Nicky Farrell.

Roslyn   Louise, sit down please. Let's discuss this calmly . . . can we? You remember what I told you about how my sister was killed?

Louise   I'd never have trusted you if you hadn't said about that. I'd never have let you use me.

Roslyn   I'm not using you. I'm working for you.

Louise   Not any more.

Roslyn   Think, Louise. Think about what I told you.
What I said we can achieve in terms of keeping Darren's
memory alive . . . and making life difficult for his killer.

Louise   Yeah, well, maybe I'm really stupid, but I just
don't see how your going clubbing with that bastard is
making things difficult for him.

Roslyn   Who do you think put the idea of phoning in to
that radio show into his head? You then had the
opportunity to provoke him into making an outburst which
has knocked his record out of the charts and got his new flat
firebombed. Did you see *that* on the news? That's teamwork,
Louise.

Louise   Why do you want to ruin him? It wasn't your
husband he killed.

Roslyn   No, but it struck a chord with my own experience
of losing my sister. I saw how the publicity from what had
happened was going to make him a star . . . and as a
publicist I felt sickened . . . while knowing I was in a position
to help you.

Louise   You're painting yourself as some kind of
superhero . . . a moral crusader . . . but it said in the paper
you were set to make his band into chart-toppers.

Roslyn   Don't believe a word you read in the papers. And
remember, you have to build them up before you can knock
them down.

Louise   How do I know it's Nicky you're planning to
knock down? How do I know it's not me?

Roslyn   Louise, I can only ask you to trust me. I can't do
more than that. Sit down, please.

Louise *sits.* **Roslyn** *reaches into her bag, pulls out a folded sheet of
fax paper. She unfolds it and shows it to* **Louise**.

Roslyn   What do you think of this?

Louise   What . . . *The Marina Walker Show* again.

Roslyn   If you're not interested . . . if you're reconsidering our relationship, I won't be offended . . . This is the figure they're offering you to appear . . .

Louise   Shit, this is ridiculous. OK, where's the catch? What do they want me to do?

Roslyn   Just be yourself . . . like when you were on there before.

Louise   They didn't offer money like this before.

Roslyn   You didn't have a publicist then. Plus, after the way you provoked Nicky Farrell on the radio, you're hot property.

Louise   So when is this . . . that they want me on the show?

Roslyn   Tomorrow afternoon.

Louise   God . . .

Roslyn   I appreciate it's short notice . . .

Louise   Well, it gives me less time to feel nervous, I suppose.

Roslyn   I've taken the liberty of booking you into the Hilton, so you won't have to rush back up to town in the morning . . .

Louise   The Hilton . . . isn't that really –

Roslyn   All paid for courtesy of the TV company.

Louise   I've nothing to wear . . . I didn't posh up to come here today . . .

Roslyn   We can go shopping, you and me, when we've eaten, have a really nice relaxing afternoon in Knightsbridge . . .

Louise   Roslyn . . . do you think my mum could come on the show with me this time? I know she's feeling a bit left out of things . . . and I'd feel less nervous if she was there beside me. You see, last time . . . I didn't know what it would involve . . . I just got all caught up in the excitement . . .

Roslyn   I'm sure it's going to be just as exciting this time around.

Louise   What I mean is that this time I'll probably be really nervous . . .

Roslyn   And of course you'd like your mum sitting there beside you? Will she be at home this afternoon?

Louise   She always stays in and does the ironing on a Thursday.

Roslyn   Well, not today. We'll send a car for her, and she'll be in time to join us for a tea somewhere.

Louise   How about the Ritz? Mum's always wanted tea at the Ritz.

Roslyn   Perfect. Right, I'll give the Hilton a bell and book your mum in, then we can hit Harrods and Harvey Nicks. Can you just pop downstairs and ask Sophie to hold all my calls?

Louise   Thanks, Roslyn. I'm sorry about what I said earlier . . .

Roslyn   It's forgotten.

Exit **Louise**.

Roslyn *takes out her mobile phone.*

Roslyn   Marina? Hi, it's Roslyn again . . . It's all set up my end. Yes, it *is* exciting, isn't it? I think you're doing a great job with publicising the show at this short notice. No, she doesn't know anything. I'm taking her shopping and got a car bringing her mum up here from Littlehampton so neither of them will have time to see the TV ad or read a paper. And I've given Nicky instructions to stay indoors. I know I am, Marina. But I think we both know it has to be

confrontational. Oh yes, it has to be a safe environment . . .
I'm having to think of the safety of both my clients here. No,
Nicky's all talk, he's not going to have a go at her physically
. . . but if he did, and I'm stating categorically that he won't,
you must have enough people there to stop him. That's fine.
Talk later, Marina. Take care.

Blackout.

Act Three

Scene One

Two separate seated areas. **Phil** *brings some coffees to the left (lit) one, where* **Nicky** *and* **Evan** *are sitting.*

Phil   It looks like we're not opening the show any more. They've changed the running order.

Nicky   So what, something else happens, then we do our first number?

Phil   They've cut our first number.

Nicky   Shit! We only get to do two songs now?

Phil   You'll still get paid for three. That's in your contract.

Nicky   That's not the fucking point.

Evan   We were opening with 'Hit and Run' and we need to plug that to get it back into this week's chart.

Nicky   We could cut 'Ain't Got No Life' and close with 'Hit and Run'.

Phil   No can do. It'll fuck up their timings. You've got to do it like you did at rehearsal.

Nicky   But with a third of our stuff cut. I'm not happy about this, Phil. I thought Roz was going to be here. I think we need her to have a word . . .

Phil   *I've* talked to the powers that be, and there's nothing they can do. We're just not the biggest story breaking today and we have to accept that.

Enter a **Harassed-Looking Person** *wearing a headset who whispers to* **Phil***.*

Phil   Look, guys . . . we've only got the closing song.

Nicky   Fucking hell!

Nicky *gets up.*

Phil   And your interview with Marina.

Evan *gets up.*

Evan   Yeah, like, why don't they cut his fucking interview? I bet that's Roslyn's doing, isn't it? Don't you see what she's trying to do, Nicky? She's trying to drive a wedge between you and us. Next thing she'll be telling you to ditch us and go solo.

Nicky   That's bollocks. Where is she? I'm going to call her.

Phil   Guys, look, sit down, please. Listen . . . I know the producer, I'm the one who used to work on this crappy show. And he's doing his best for us.

Evan   I'm just saying we could do the song instead of Nicky's interview with Marina.

Nicky   No way. Look, Evan, it's not cos I want to be bigger than the band. It's nothing like that. If I don't get the chance to say to Marina I'm sorry about what I said on Chat Radio, the album's not going to get back into the charts, is it?

Phil   He's right, Evan. Look, I had a pretty hectic meeting with the suits at the record company. They may no longer be right behind us if Nicky doesn't apologise on air for his remarks about drugs and driving.

Nicky   At least I won't have to mention Louise fucking Fielder.

Phil   See, the way the company sees it, they paid out a big signing fee, then they've spent thousands promoting a single and an album that hardly any radio stations will play. So right now Alice Don't Surf is a liability, and there are those in the organisation who see the quickest way of ending this crisis is by parting company with the band. It's fucking bad luck that this royal scandal should break today of all days, but Marina is of course a close friend of the royals . . .

Nicky   And are you a close friend of the royals too?

Phil   Don't take it out on me. I'm on your team now.

Evan   For how long? Until the ship starts sinking?

Phil   This ship isn't going to sink.

Lights up on the other side of the stage as **Roslyn** *explains the situation to* **Louise** *and* **Elsa**. **Louise** *looks very nervous.*

Roslyn   . . . anything to do with the royal family will increase the viewing figures tenfold.

Elsa   So my daughter's playing second fiddle to Princess Di? Hasn't that woman had more than her fair share of publicity?

Roslyn   It's just the way things are. Fairness doesn't come into it. All we can do is sit tight and wait until you're called.

Elsa *looks at the telly.*

Elsa   Who's that Marina's talking to at the moment?

Roslyn   Megan Fetter-Brown – she's a royal commentator.

Elsa   I'm sure I could be one of those. All you have to do is go on telly and speculate about what it all means, if Andrew meets Fergie's eyes, or Di's dressed in green.

Roslyn   The thing Megan has, or says she has, of course much of it may be bluff and luck, is insider information. Servants at the palace talk to her.

Louise *takes a sip of water from a glass on the table.*

Louise   I feel really nervous.

Roslyn   It'll be fine.

Louise   I'm not used to all this waiting about.

Elsa *puts her hand on* **Louise**'s *knee*.

Louise   You know, I think after this show . . . I just want to go home and concentrate on getting my self-help group off the ground . . .

Roslyn   Being on here this afternoon will bring you loads of prospective members. You'll probably be able to set up a nationwide network straight away. And once your book's out, you'll be able to reach out even further . . .

Louise   I don't know . . . I've been having second thoughts about my book . . .

Roslyn   Which is already half-written . . . and the writer's really looking forward to showing you the first draft . . .

Louise   I'm not sure it's right to cash in any more from Darren's death.

Roslyn   We can look at turning the group into a charity . . . then those who most need help will benefit, while keeping Darren's memory alive.

Louise   I wouldn't forget Darren if I called a halt to all of this. I'd have time to remember him again . . .

Roslyn   I entirely sympathise, Louise. Of course you're feeling a little tired and confused right now . . .

Elsa   I do think Louise has been working too hard . . .

Roslyn   And it's all becoming a little bit much, I know. But after today we'll sit down and rethink our whole strategy . . . I've been chatting with Justine, you remember her at *Women Now*? She's interested in the possibility of you having your own column in the magazine, just talking about day-to-day life in a chalet park on the River Arun . . .

Louise   Nothing much happens.

Roslyn   It doesn't have to be *strictly* factual. You can make up some eccentric characters who live on the river, I'm sure. Their staff writers will help you. If the 'People on the River' column is a success, we could probably take a similar format to the radio, or sell the idea for a TV series.

The **Harassed-Looking Person** *with the headset comes in and whispers to* **Roslyn**.

Roslyn   No, no, we don't mind waiting. We understand of course. They're going live to an OB at Buckingham Palace.

Elsa   The Duke of Edinburgh?

Louise   OB stands for outside broadcast, Mum.

Roslyn   Basically, we're going to have to wait a bit longer.

Louise   Oh no.

Roslyn (*to the* **Harassed-Looking Person**)   Can we have some refreshments here?

Exit the **Harassed-Looking Person**.

Louise   Will they still have time to interview me?

Roslyn   It might be a shortened format.

Louise   I hope so. I don't know how I'm going to get my words out.

Roslyn   Try to relax, Louise.

Elsa   It can't be as bad as last time. At least you'll have another chance to mention the group . . . without being face-to-face with that evil young man . . .

Roslyn   I'll go and see if there's any news on when we'll be on.

Exit **Roslyn**.

Louise   I don't know if I can do this, Mum.

On the other side of the room, the **Harassed-Looking Person** *comes in and whispers intently to* **Phil**.

Nicky (*to* **Evan**)　Are you thinking what I'm thinking? If it means no fucking songs, I'm walking, interview or no interview.

Phil (*to the* **Harassed-Looking Person**)　Any chance of some beers here?

Exit the **Harassed-Looking Person**.

Phil　Hey, listen, guys, it's just another *small* delay. No need to lose it just yet, right?

Nicky　I think I'll go outside for a bit.

Phil　Free beer is on its way.

Nicky　I need some fresh air.

Phil　Don't wander too far.

Exit **Nicky**.

Phil　He's a bit wired-up, today. I wish this wasn't a live show . . .

Evan　Where are these drinks then?

The **Harassed-Looking Person** *puts some drinks and nibbles in front of* **Elsa** *and* **Louise**.

Elsa　They make these chairs too comfy, don't they? Can't be good for your posture.

Louise　No Twiglets . . .

The **Harassed-Looking Person** *takes beers and nibbles to* **Phil** *and* **Evan**.

Phil　No Twiglets.

Louise *turns on the telly. On-screen,* **Marina** *is interviewing a* **Megan Fetter-Brown**.

Megan　Oh ya, the family will come bouncing back from this crisis, I'm sure. You know, they're made of stern stuff, stiff upper lip, all rally round in times of trouble.

Marina   Ring in now, and tell us whether you are behind or against the Queen on this issue.

Louise *turns off the television.*

Elsa   I'd like to know what the Queen Mother thinks. She's the only one with any sense.

Enter **Roslyn** *to where* **Phil** *and* **Evan** *are sitting.*

Roslyn   Hello, boys.

Phil   I think Nicky's gone looking for you.

Roslyn   There's nothing I can do, unfortunately.

Evan   That's just what we told him.

Phil   I wouldn't be surprised to see us sent home without getting on the show at all.

Roslyn *checks her watch.*

Roslyn   It's not looking good.

Evan   Shit, what a waste of bloody time.

Roslyn   Of course, you'll be paid whatever.

Evan   I should fucking hope so.

Evan *gets up.*

Phil   And where are you –

Evan   Need a piss.

Exit **Evan**.

Roslyn   So how's Marina?

Phil   Eh?

Roslyn   Well, aren't you and she . . .

Phil   Who told you . . . ?

Roslyn   We're old friends, Phil. Locker-room chat and all that.

On the other side of the stage, **Louise** *and* **Elsa** *are talking.*

Elsa   I'd be livid if we've come all the way up here . . . to be sent back home again. And it was my WI afternoon.

Louise   I shouldn't have let them drag you up here.

Elsa   Don't be silly, you need some moral support.

Louise   I feel a bit sick.

Elsa   It's just butterflies in your stomach.

Louise   Yeah, well, I don't think they're gonna stay there much longer.

Enter the **Harassed-Looking Person**.

Harassed-Looking Person   We're ready for you in the next five minutes. Can you come back through to the studio, Louise?

Louise   At bloody last.

Louise *and* **Elsa** *get up.*

Harassed-Looking Person   No, just Louise for the moment. I'll come back for you, Elsa.

The **Harassed-Looking Person** *escorts* **Louise** *front of stage and leaves her.*

Enter **Marina**.

Marina   Louise, how wonderful to see you again! We're currently with the outside broadcast, then there's a break, then we're on. It's been such a hectic day. This stuff about the princess breaking *now*. I do really feel for her, don't you? She's not had it easy. (*Into her earpiece.*) . . . Where is he?

Louise   Marina . . . Can I be excused for a minute? I need the loo.

Louise *walks front of stage to exit.*

Marina   What? You need to pee? Be quick. (*Into earpiece.*) No, I don't want him on set for another ten minutes, but he should be waiting back there. He needs to hear what she has to say. (*Pause.*) Well, for fuck's sake, find him. Now.

Louise *looks back at* **Marina**, *and the brightly lit area front of stage as she exits, and walks straight into* **Nicky**.

Louise   Shit!

Nicky   What the fuck are you doing here? . . . I get it – you thought you'd slip into the audience . . . and try to fuck up my interview?

Louise   . . . You're on the show?

Nicky   And you're not, so I don't know what you're doing here. I'm not having you in the building while I'm on air . . . I'm calling security right now and watching you thrown out on your fat arse.

Louise   It's *my* interview, I'm on with Marina, straight after the OB. You're not on this show. No one told me you'd be here.

Nicky   Looks like nobody told either of us. Fucking hell.

Louise   You're not being on there, you're not being on there with me! I hate you. I fucking hate you! You killed my husband! You fucking bastard!

Louise *attacks* **Nicky**. *They fight.*

Enter **Evan**. *He pulls* **Nicky** *and* **Louise** *apart.* **Louise** *leans back against the wall, sobbing.*

Evan   She's on the show too?

Nicky   Go out front, hail a fucking cab. We're out of here.

Evan   Just you leave her. Leave her, right?

Exit **Evan**.

Nicky   You can have your fucking interview all to yourself. You can go on there and say anything you want about me. I don't give a fuck. Nobody gives a fuck.

Louise   I'm not going on. I'm not going on. You've ruined my life.

Nicky   You've fucked up *my* life. You and your husband, you stupid bitch.

Louise *tries to hit* **Nicky**. *He catches her hand. They start fighting again.*

Enter **Evan** *with his rifle. He points it straight at them.*

Evan   Break it up. Now!

The gun goes off. **Louise** *falls on the floor.*

Nicky   Oh fuck, Evan. Jesus Christ . . .

Evan   I'll get help.

Nicky   Evan . . . don't leave me with . . .

Exit **Evan**.

Nicky *bends over* **Louise**.

Nicky   If you're dead . . . oh fuck this . . .

He walks away, then looks back. He goes back to **Louise**.

Louise.

Louise *moans, starts to come to.*

Nicky   Louise . . . Oh, come on, somebody! Louise, are you OK?

Louise *drags herself up, stumbles.* **Nicky** *steadies her.*

Nicky   Steady. Did you hit your head? It's all right. It's OK now.

Louise *leans on* **Nicky** *as he slowly leads her off.*

Elsa *walks front of stage from the seating area. An alarm goes off.*

Elsa   Louise!

Enter **Roslyn**.

Where's my daughter?

Roslyn   I'm not quite sure . . . there seems to be some kind of security alert . . . a gunman in the building, so somebody says.

Elsa   Where's Louise? Louise!

Exit **Elsa**.

Marina (*off*)   Roslyn!

Enter **Marina**.

Fuck your fucking clients, Roslyn. That's my programme totally fucked.

Roslyn   Only the last half-hour.

Marina   They've switched to bloody *Bugs Bunny*.

Roslyn   I don't suppose anyone'll notice.

Marina   Fuck you, you cunt.

Roslyn   Marina! – it's not my fault . . .

Marina   It's that military maniac gone on the rampage . . . he's one of your bloody clients.

Roslyn   Evan isn't my client, I'm only Nicky and Louise's publicist. The band's manager's responsible for Evan . . . Phil, your boyfriend . . .

Enter **Phil** (*unnoticed by* **Roslyn** *and* **Marina**).

Marina   My what? I don't know what you're talking about . . . me and that greasy little ex-floor manager, don't be so –

Phil *pushes past them and exits. Pause, as they watch him depart.*

Marina   I tell you, I'm never having anything else to do with you, Roslyn, or any of your so-called clients. You're history as far as *The Marina Walker Show* is concerned and when I've talked to a few of my friends, you won't even be history.

Roslyn   Marina . . . I know mistakes have been made . . .

Marina   You're full of shit . . .

Roslyn   But accidents happen, and we can move on.

Evan *rushes through with his rifle.*

Roslyn   Now who do you think's going to be on all tomorrow's front pages? Go on, who?

Marina   Princess fucking Di – I don't know.

Roslyn   Who would give you even better viewing figures than today? And everyone's sure to want to know what put *The Marina Walker Show* off the air . . .

Enter **Evan**.

Roslyn   And hear the story of the man who ran amok on prime-time TV . . .

She takes **Evan***'s arm.*

Roslyn   Tomorrow night's guest, Evan.

Blackout.

Scene Two

The curtains slowly fall away to reveal the singed walls and blackened windows of **Nicky***'s burnt-out flat.*

Enter **Nicky** *and* **Louise***, slowly, almost dazed.*

Louise   It reeks of smoke in here.

Nicky *picks up the phone.*

Louise   What are you doing?

Nicky *unplugs the phone.* **Louise** *sits down on a chair, turned away from him.*

Louise   They'll all come here . . . Roslyn, Marina, the reporters.

Nicky   The doorbell doesn't work any more . . .

Louise   They'll find me . . .

Pause.

Nicky   Look, Louise, I'm –

Louise (*interrupting*)   Don't talk. There's been too much talking . . .

Pause.

Nicky   OK?

Louise *does not move.*

Nicky   Are you OK?

Pause.

Louise   Yeah.

Nicky   I'm sorry.

Pause. He approaches her.

Louise . . .

He crouches beside her.

. . . I didn't want it to happen. Can you understand that?

He tries to take her arm, she moves to push him away, but does not.

Any of this . . . this thing we've been caught up in . . .

Pause. She sobs softly.

It's all right . . . hey, it's all right. It's over now . . . It's finished.

Pause.

Louise   I miss him.

She looks at **Nicky**.

Every day . . . I miss him.

Louise   I'm truly sorry.

Fade in traffic sounds from outside.

Louise   It isn't enough.

Nicky   It's all there is.

Blackout.

Know Your Rights

Know Your Rights was first performed at the Red Room, Battersea Arts Centre, London, on 8 May 1998. The cast was as follows:

Jane   Frances Cuka
Bonnie   Noma Dumezweni

Directed by Lisa Goldman
Designed by Rosalind Coombes
Costumes by Alex Buxton
Lighting by Neil Sloan
Sound by Yvonne Gilbert
Assistant Director Lucy Whitton

Jane, *aged fifty-nine, has her right arm encased in plaster. She sits reading* Woman's Weekly. **Bonnie** *is also on stage, sitting down. A tape of Edith Piaf plays 'Milord'. Suddenly the tape goes wobbly.*

Jane   Oh.

Pause.

Damn.

She stops the tape, takes it out, peers at it.

Looks all right. Not all come out at least. I hate that. You stick a pen through one of the little wheels and wind it all back in again. Next thing you know, the bloody stuff's in a tangle and you can't even get the little door open.

She puts the tape back, plays a bit.

I'm sure that's not right. I don't much like her at the best of times, but she does stick to the tune, usually.

She stops the tape.

It'll have to go back. Pity. I was going to take it in to Simon this afternoon. Hope they're all right about changing it.

She tries to open a bottle of sherry.

Bugger.

She tries again.

Isn't it stupid? I can't do anything. I think I can . . . get dinner, do the washing one-handed, but then when it comes to opening things, chopping things, lifting a pan off the gas it's bloody useless. I wonder if I could ask Frank downstairs . . . just to open this and a couple of tins. In normal circumstances, I'd rather go ask *her* . . . up there. But I can't, not now. The solicitor's advised me against having any contact with her. For now. Until I've made a decision about what to do.

She gets the bottle open.

Bingo. Ow. Oh bugger. That hurts. Trouble with Frank is he's got ideas. About him and me. 'We're both in the same situation, you and me,' that's what he said. But he means because his poor wife's passed on. I thought he'd made a mistake – got hold of the wrong end of the stick. 'Oh but I'm not a widow,' I told him, 'I still have my Simon, thank God.' And he says, 'I suppose I just meant, that in our different ways we're both alone.' 'Alone!' I said to Simon. 'How can I be alone while we've still got each other?' He didn't say anything. But I know he understood.

Pause.

I know he did.

She manages to open the bottle, pours a glass of sherry, sips it through the next speech.

I don't drink. Not unless I've got company. My boss was very understanding . . . said he'd look forward to having me back, just as soon as I'm out of plaster . . . even though I'm really only a temporary now. Hopefully it'll only be a couple of weeks . . . the plasterer – you know the girl who put this on – 'plaster-person', would you call her? Anyway, whatever, she said it'd probably have to stay on for a month, but then she's not a doctor, is she? Have to wait 'til I see the specialist, Monday.

She pours another drink.

So as I said, four hours I was sitting around up there, and the only magazines they'd got to read was one copy of *Country Life*, from December 1992, and a couple of those dreadful rubbishy things full of sex. Well, I soon flicked through those. And then the time really began to drag. There were all kinds sitting around the waiting area – bandages and blood like you can't imagine. I hope they were seeing the little ones first. I mean, it's worse for the kids. Us old 'uns at least know they'll get to us eventually.

Pause.

With a bit of luck anyway.

Anyway as I was sitting there, with the rest of the walking wounded, I started to read all the posters on the wall. Things like 'What to do in an emergency' – stupid really, as by the time you're reading the bloody thing, you've already managed to get yourself to casualty.

Then I see this leaflet from a firm of solicitors, about making a personal injury claim. Don't get me wrong, I mean, I don't want to sue the poor girl or anything. An accident's an accident, after all. But if I'm going to lose up to a month's wages . . . well, I've got to think about things.

Bonnie I know it sounds awful, but my only thoughts were for Jake. Whether he was hurt. It was like I didn't even see her lying there. Not straight away. Jake was bawling, and I just rushed to the bottom of the stairs, to scoop him up, to hold him . . . Those concrete stairs. I couldn't believe he hadn't smashed his head open. I couldn't believe he was fine. Completely OK.

She kind of groaned. And that's when I noticed her. Or when I was able to think about her being there. Mrs . . . you know, I can never remember names. The woman from upstairs, anyway. Jake must've banged into her, tripped her up. He always wants to run down the stairs. He's a bundle of energy. And cooped up in a flat with nowhere to let off steam. Normally I've got hold of his hand, but I was carrying his little trike. We were going to the park. That's our Tuesday afternoon treat. Get a bag of peanuts from Safeway, sit in the park and feed the squirrels.

She insisted on trying to get up, and I couldn't stop her. She said she felt sick, and she was really pale. Pale and shaking. She gripped on to the banister, saying she was OK, but I kept hold of her, just the same. I was so scared she'd fall down the rest of the stairs. I shouted to Jake to sit down at the bottom, and he went and sat there, crossed-legged like at playgroup.

Course she wouldn't hear of me dialing 999. 'I'm not that bad. I'll be OK.' I don't know why I didn't just go and call an ambulance anyway. I suppose I was feeling so guilty about Jake knocking her down, that I didn't want to risk making her angry. So I said I'd get her a taxi. She protested about that too. But then she tried to take a step, leaning on the banister and she kind of collapsed. It was her arm. She said OK, I could call her a taxi.

Fuck. Shit, why am I so stupid? I called her a taxi. And I didn't pay for it, did I? Didn't think about it. I'm not good in emergencies. I'm the first to admit it. I said I'd go with her but she said she was sure she was OK. 'No bones broken,' she said. No fucking bones broken. Then I wake up in this morning and *this* is on the doorstep.

Bonnie *waves a white envelope.*

Jane   I don't want any trouble. I don't like any unpleasantness. Lived here for . . . it must be nearly ten years now. Yes, ten years come July. It's a nice friendly block. But not too friendly . . . not one of those places where everyone knows everyone else's business. Here, when you see your neighbours, they say hello, nod or smile. If you get somebody else's post by accident, you take it round, and they say thanks . . . maybe invite you in for a cuppa . . . you thank them very much, but you say you can't stop. And they know you're going to say that. Because you don't want to put them to any trouble. And they were only offering out of politeness, see?

Bonnie   I went to the Citizens' Advice . . . It's a Dunkin' Donut now. Funny how you don't notice things being closed 'til you need them. I've been thumbing through the phone book all morning. There must be somewhere I can go for advice.

I hate it here. It gets me down sometimes. I know I should think myself lucky. It's not a bad flat . . . and most people I know've only got bedsits. Jake has a nice big bedroom, and

I've not had anyone complaining when he's noisy, and he is sometimes.

It's a shame there's no younger people in the place though. No one else with kids. Not that I've anything against the oldies. They've never given me any trouble, until now. When I moved in, must've been last March . . . the old bloke on the ground floor, and . . . what's-his-name . . . (*She checks the letter.*) . . . Mr Edison, the husband of the one that's giving me all this hassle, he helped me carry my stuff up here. He seemed quite normal then. Still holding it together.

Jane   She's single parent, like so many of them are. Of course I don't know her circumstances. And I'm not judgemental . . . though I think it's a good idea if they can get some of them back to work.

Mind you, I don't really see anything wrong with bringing up a child on your own. Not when you look at the young men of today. I mean, there're still a few decent ones out there . . . but they're few and far between.

Bonnie   I went to the library. It was still there. And it still smells the same. Like TCP. The librarian had a queue of kids wanting stuff about the Millennium Dome. Must be for their homework, and I could see it was gonna keep her busy for hours, so I wandered about until I found a shelf marked 'Law'. There's so many kinds of law . . . and I didn't know. I mean, shit . . . I thought there'd be one book that'd tell me everything I need to know. It's times like this when you really realise how stupid you are . . . how little they bothered to teach you at school.

I took every book off that fucking shelf and I started to go through 'em one by one. You can only take four out at a time, and so I'd gotta pick the best ones . . .

You know. I don't even know if it's a criminal or civil case . . . Or something else again. The more I read the more confused I got. Fuck this, I thought. Just pick four by doing eenie, meenie, minie, mo. So that's how I ended up with *A*

Guide to Civil Law – well a three-year-old can't be a criminal can he? And I got *Law Made Simple*, one called *Know Your Rights*, and *Green Eggs and Ham* . . . for Jake. Got some music tapes out too . . . they've a few quite pop ones – but weird stuff like Björk, and the Throwing Muses. Maybe that's what young librarians are into.

I meant to read all the books last night, but I wound up dropping off to sleep before I'd even finished *Green Eggs and Ham*. I wish they'd taught us something about law at school. It's the same with dealing with banks and benefits – if they just covered a bit of stuff like that in maths lessons. Would've been more useful than fucking co-sines and tangents. I know education's like everything else – you get what you pay for. And if you can't pay you get shite . . . I don't want Jake to end up like me – I want him to be able to make something of himself. I'm gonna make sure he can read before he starts school.

There's a solicitor in the high street offering an hour free – just to go in and talk about your problem. I'm just worried I won't explain it properly, or they'll think I'm in the wrong.

Jane   I've still got the first photos I took of Simon. It was at some work do . . . someone's leaving party, I think. There's one shot of everyone else, and all the rest are of Simon. I was that gone on him, even then. I'd only been working there for a couple of months, and his office was on the other side of the building. Saw him every day in the canteen, but he never sat on my table. He had to sit with the other section supervisors of course. Things were more . . . formal then. Nowadays I can sit at the same table as my boss and nobody bats an eye. The classless society, they call it. Course it doesn't mean we're taking home the same pay as them . . .

It was being such a bright spark that was Simon's downfall really . . . he worked all the overtime imaginable, never took a day off sick. Well, finally he gets his reward – promotion to management level . . . I was so proud. By that time of

course I was at home with the kids. Then all of a sudden
they were cutting down staff – and it was the managers they
said they'd too many of. Simon got a good redundancy
package, but with two young children that didn't go far.
Eventually, he got another job – as a van driver, but his
heart was never in it. Then a few years ago, I saw in the
paper an ad for part-time temporaries. And when I went to
apply, I found it was at the old place, working on the packer
– so there I am back doing my old job, like before I left and
had the kids. But less hours and less money. And of course
no sick pay.

When we sold our house and moved here, we'd quite a nice
little nest egg, our 'rainy day' money, Simon used to call it.
But it never rains, it pours, doesn't it?

Bonnie   A couple of months after I moved in, I woke
one night to knocking on my door. I was a bit nervous like,
but I've a door-chain so I opened it a crack. And it was
Mr . . . . . . the husband of the woman upstairs . . . standing
there. 'Janie. Janie,' he says. 'You're on the wrong floor,' I
told him. Thought maybe he'd had a few drinks, but he's
still just standing there, looking at me. Eventually, I had to
take him down to her.

Jane   He seems a nice kiddie . . . I was so relieved he
wasn't hurt. She should've been holding his hand walking
down the stairs. I always did with our two. You can't trust a
little one like that to walk down on his own.

Bonnie   A few weeks later the police brought him back. I
saw the flashing light outside, and them helping him from
the car. Soaked to the skin he was, and it wasn't raining.

After that I didn't see him around any more. I think she had
to put him in a home. He's quite a lot older than her, I'd
say.

Jane   My solicitor thinks I should mention my concerns
about the kiddie. I'm sure the girl cares about him. And is a
good mother. Usually.

Georgina . . . the solicitor, is sure we're going to win. The catch is I can't get legal aid because technically I've still got a job . . . even if I'm not going to be earning for the next six weeks at least. The specialist was sure about that. Six weeks in plaster. And I can't work the packer one-handed.

Simon's care is really expensive. It's private, the place he's in, and it's small and very nice . . . as nice as one of those places is ever going to be. They have activities, and he seems . . . well no worse at least since he's been there. And that to me makes it worth the expense . . . but I hope this legal business can be settled quickly . . . and I can win enough damages to make sure Simon can still have the best care available. I've written to Richard, my son in Australia . . . I don't like to ask him for money directly . . . so I've just kind of hinted that it would be OK for him to offer.

Bonnie   My solicitor's got kids . . . he was all right . . . we sat chatting . . . he told me all about his daughter . . . she's only nine, and she's already an expert violin player. I was telling him about Jake and his little keyboard . . . then suddenly I noticed the clock on the wall. We'd used up nearly thirty minutes of my free hour of legal advice, just chatting! But finally it was OK, cos apparently I can get legal aid . . . as I'm on the income support. He's going to sort it all out – says I can leave it to him.

Jane   So I get a letter from her solicitor – 'Our client has been granted legal aid. My solicitor says that's because she's unemployed.'

Pause.

But I'm not so sure she is. I mean, she goes out, Thursday, Friday and Saturdays, at about five o'clock, taking the kiddie with her. According to Frank. He doesn't have much to do but watch other people's comings and goings. Poor old sod. He said I could always rely on him. He invited me in. I only stopped for a minute . . . well, ten minutes. He made us a cuppa and got out the date and walnut. 'Sit yourself down,' he said. But I wasn't sitting on the settee with him, oh no. And I kept mentioning Simon's name. After a bit, he got the message.

Frank said he'd always fancied being a detective. It'd be like being Inspector Morse, he said. He's going to follow her this evening and see where she works. About eight, there's this knock on the door. Frank. With the collar of his coat turned up like he's Sam Spade. I didn't let him in, not at that time of night. But what he had to say was interesting . . . She works up the new Safeway.

Bonnie Just had the DSS on the phone. I've got to go in and see them. You usually just get a letter if it's about the Restart, or some other scheme, so it's got me a bit worried.

Jane It's been a bit of a depressing day. Had to go up the hospital and have my cast taken off. Well, the X-rays showed it hasn't healed properly . . . the bones haven't knitted together right. So back on with the plaster, and he says it may need an operation. To put a pin in it. Why they couldn't have done that straight away I don't know. And he couldn't tell me when I can go back to work. I'm getting a bit worried. The solicitor's bill's in the high hundreds already . . . and she says that because that girl's got legal aid, they're not likely to want it quickly settled. I'm wondering whether this whole thing was a bad idea. I said that to Georgina – the solicitor. She says she's confident I'll win a tidy sum, but how am I going to live in the meantime? And pay Simon's care fees?

Bonnie The DSS inspector calls me into her office. And closes the door. Then she tells me they've received information that I've got a job. They've been informed wrong, I tell them. Or it's a mistake. She says they know I work up Safeway three nights a week, and alternate Saturdays. One of their snoopers has followed me to work. And Safeway's have fucking admitted to employing me. Well, had no choice really, did they?

They had to sack me too.

I told the DSS, that I'd only done it 'cos of needing the money for Jake. They're always cutting my income support and housing . . . by the odd quid here and there, and it probably seems like nothing to them, but how do you tell a boy of three, he can't have another box of juice, or Kinder egg this week? I said I'd pay it all back – the money I claimed while I was working. I don't know where I would've got it . . . I was just panicking. I can't really remember half of what I said. I think I started shouting, and then I was in tears. The DSS inspector gave me a tissue. She said she understood how easy it was to get into this kind of mess. She's got kids herself.

But they're still gonna prosecute.

This time I think it's criminal law. Making a fraudulent benefit claim is what they call it. But that's not how it is. I mean, I wasn't working when I signed on. It's only keep having my money cut that's made me have to get a job as well. She asked why I hadn't taken a full-time job at Safeway's, and signed off. But I can't afford to pay someone to mind Jake full-time . . . and I wouldn't want to. I'd miss out on so much, if I couldn't spend any time with him.

They've stopped all my benefits for the moment. And the rent's due this week. I can't see the landlords being very understanding. A month back, my housing cheque went astray. I phoned them straight away about it, but they still sent me a letter threatening to evict me.

Jane   Sometimes when I go to see Simon, he says, 'Let's sit out in the garden' . . . so he must think we're still at our previous home. All the same, I'm not moving him to just anywhere.

I looked at quite a few council-run places, before coming to a decision. They're all much bigger than the home where he is now. And only for people with Alzheimer's. There aren't as many staff as I'd like there to be, and at a couple of them, the patients were left wandering unsupervised. At the first place I went there was an awful smell, like somebody had

. . . soiled themselves. I mentioned it to one of the assistants, and she just ignored me. So I was out of there, like a shot.

The one I eventually chose was a bit more cheerful. Well, the nurse who showed me round seemed nice enough . . . And it's only temporary after all, until I can get hold of some money. Richard's in a tight spot himself at the moment, financially, but he might be able to help me out in a month or two. With that, and as long I can win compensation for all the time I'm having to take off work, hopefully Simon'll soon be able to go back to the old place.

Bonnie   Another night with no fucking sleep. I know my court hearing about the benefit thing's still weeks away, and the business with Mrs Edison might not even come to court . . . that's if I believe my lawyer. He doesn't seem too worried . . . but then it's not him with his benefits stopped, and his landlord getting arsy.

I'd take a couple of sleepers, if I wasn't scared of not hearing Jake if he calls out in the night. If I didn't have Jake, I'd probably take the whole fucking bottle.

Jane   I went with Simon in the minibus. I thought he'd be excited to see the outside world again . . . but he didn't even want to look out the window. His mouth kept moving, as though he wanted to speak but he didn't say anything.

When we got there I stayed with him for a little while, to help him settle in. I played him Edith Piaf, and he sang the 'nons' in 'Je Ne Regrette Rien'. Then I ask him if he likes his new room. He just wants to sing. 'Non!' I ask him if he knows where he is. 'Where are we, Simon?' 'Home,' he says. 'Our home, Janie.' 'Janie.' He said my name. That's the first time in months he's said my name.

Bonnie   I slapped Jake. I've never ever done that before. Never. It wasn't his fault. Just he was making a noise . . .

I hate myself. How could I hit him? How could I get our lives in this mess?

This bloody, shitty mess.

I rang my social worker. Didn't tell her I hit Jake. I mean, I couldn't. You can't trust 'em. She kept saying that things would be OK . . . she says I should go out and try to forget my troubles. I didn't like to say that there's nowhere I can go without any money. Until the DSS sort out my emergency payment, I can't go spending on anything. I don't feel like phoning them about it. And I can't force myself to go in there, with them all looking at me like I'm a criminal or something.

Every day I wait for a cheque to arrive. Every day all I get is fucking solicitors' letters. From the old bag's solicitor, the DSS's solicitor, or my solicitor, saying he's been in touch with the other two. Oh and I got a bill from Cable and Wireless. The gas and leccy can't be far behind.

If I can't pay my bills . . . and my fines . . .

. . . I mean, there's no way I could go to prison, surely . . . It couldn't happen, could it? Not when I've got a kid.

Jane   I got back from visiting Simon, and I popped in to see Frank. He's really been so kind. I only meant to be a minute, but he was just making a bite to eat and it would've been rude to refuse.

Then I look at my watch and it's past eight o'clock. So we have one for the road, and I'm on my way back upstairs, when I come face-to-face with that girl. I tried to look away, waiting for her to pass me. Well, my solicitor says I should avoid any contact with her for the present. And her one's probably told her something similar. Or should've done.

. . . I've never heard such language in all my . . . *venomous*, it was. That's the only word for it. Venomous. She must be not all there in her head or something. All the crazy things she was accusing me of.

I stood there and took it. I know I should've just walked off. I should've gone in my flat and locked the door. But you don't expect someone to start . . . abusing you in your own place. Afterwards my legs were like jelly.

Frank says I should've called the police. I suppose it's too late now. They probably won't want to know anyway. I'm going to contact our landlord though. I think it's my duty to inform them if one of their tenants is causing a problem.

Bonnie   I quite often leave doing my shopping until late into the evening. I sleep better after a good shop, and so does Jake. Anyway I'm lugging my carrier bags up the stairs. Jake's run on ahead, and he's playing with his tractor on our doormat. Suddenly I hear a kind of wailing . . . then I realise it's her, Mrs Edison, coming up the stairs. And she's not wailing, she's *singing* . . . in French or something. Pissed as a fart. Honest to God.

I told my social worker . . . and she asked me was Mrs Edison pissed the day Jake tripped her up. I said I didn't think so . . . but I have seen her a bit tight other times, so who knows. I got to thinking, if she was drunk that day, then it puts her in the wrong, doesn't it? I rang my lawyer. He thinks it's a good point.

Jane   I'm writing to my MP. I don't even know if we're still Labour or gone Liberal. But Frank says there's supposed to be this thing now that if you've got bad neighbours you can have them moved away. One of the things that attracted Simon and me to this flat when we moved in was that there were only people like us . . . *quiet* people . . . working people . . . no single mothers, or anyone on the dole . . .

Bonnie   I've looked at it all ways, and I can't see another answer. I know she can't have me thrown out on the street. I know my rights . . . well, some of them. But I can't deal with all this shit. I just can't deal with it any more. I don't want to take it out on Jake. And I have been – shouting and making him stay in his room. I haven't hit him again, thank God. And I'm not gonna let it come to that. The more I think about it, the more I can see it's the only answer. Maybe I'm a coward, but I've never been a fighter.

Jane　I've had so much to sort out . . . going to see my solicitor, writing to my landlord and my MP, having tests up the hospital, before they operate on my arm . . . trying to sort out my sickness benefit claim . . . today was the first day this week I've had time to go in and see Simon.

Bonnie　I've been packing all morning. But I've only one case, and a couple of bags . . . that's all I can carry, so loads of stuff's gonna have to be left behind.

Jane　He didn't know me. Didn't even seem to realise someone was there. The nurse just shrugged. Said it was nothing unusual. How would she know. He's only been in there a week. At the old place, he'd smile the moment I entered the room. And when I took his hand, he'd squeeze it . . . and even if he couldn't talk to me . . . I'd know that he was still there . . . Despite the confusion, he was still *there*, he was still my Simon.

And now I can't reach him.

Bonnie　I've been putting off ringing my social worker. But what else can I do?

What else can I do?

Jane　They'd left him sitting there in his pyjamas. Hadn't even got him dressed. He was shivering. I had to put my coat around him. Some of his things were missing – his flannel, his spare glasses and the Piaf tape.

They wouldn't call the doctor, so I called him myself. Hours and hours I sat beside Simon. He wouldn't speak, he wouldn't eat or drink. The nurse said it didn't matter. She was very short with me.

Finally the doctor arrived. He said it was just something that happened with 'these kinds of patients'. It wasn't really medical. Maybe it was some kind of trauma brought on by the move from the private home. Then I felt awful . . .

I told Simon I'd stop the legal action, told him I'd try and get the DSS to hurry up with sickness benefit claim . . . then soon as I get some money, any money, I'll get him moved back into the old place. I'm going to try phoning my MP, I'm going to try talking to the bank manager, I'm going to start looking for somewhere cheaper to live.

I'll get things sorted out. I've always paid my taxes, I've always given to charity. I've always voted Labour . . . and Liberal . . . There'll be somewhere or someone who'll help. I told Simon not to worry.

Bonnie   Social services are gonna look after Jake. Just for a few days . . . or a week or so. Just until I can find another flat. There's plenty of flats and bedsits round here. Lots of them advertised in the paper-shop window. The problem's paying the deposit, of course.

Don't know where I'm gonna sleep tonight yet. Don't really want to spend the last of my cash on a grotty B and B. Maybe I'll just sit in the twenty-four-hour café . . . then go down the housing as soon as it opens. They've got to help me. They can't leave me like this.

I've told Jake he's just gonna have a little holiday. We always watch *The Holiday Programme*. He's quite excited, poor kid. He thinks I'm coming with him . . . and I can't bring myself to tell him. Not yet. Poor kid.

Jane (*drinking*)   I went to Woolies. It's only down the road from where Simon is. I bought another Piaf tape and took it in to him. He didn't move or make a sound as she started singing. His eyes were still empty. But I know he was listening.

I know he was listening.